Ninety Days To The God Habit

Breaking the Cycle of Mediocre Christianity

By J. Traveler Pelton

Potpourri Publishing
Mt Vernon, OH 43050

Copyright page

Ninety Days to the God Habit

Copyright© 2019 by J. Traveler Pelton

All Rights reserved. No part of this book may be reproduced in any form or by any electronic or mechanical means including information and retrievable systems without permission from the publisher/author, except by a reviewer who may quote brief passages in a review.

Published by Potpourri Publishing

Edited by Write Useful

Book cover by RebecaCovers

Printed in the United States of America

First Edition June 2019

Books> non-fiction>Christian>religious>adult

ISBN: 9781070981529

All Scripture texts quoted are from the New King James Version, copy write 1982, Thomas Nelson.

Other Books by Traveler Pelton

Spiritual Works
- God Wanted to Write a Bestseller
- Big God, Little Me
- Lenten Stories for God's Little Children
- Natural Morning
- Ninety Days to The God Habit

Christian Literary Science Fiction

The First Oberllyn Family Trilogy: The Past
- The Oberllyn's Overland: 1855-1862
- Terrorists, Traitors and Spies 1900-1990
- Rebooting the Oberllyn's 2015-2020

The Second Oberllyn Family Trilogy: The Present
- The Infant Conspiracy
- Kai Dante's Stratagem
- The Obligation of Being Oberllyn

The Third Oberllyn Family Trilogy: The Future
- To Protect One's Own
- The Importance of Family Ties
- Kith and Kin, Together Again

Family History
- Journey to Springhaven

In Collaboration with T. Bear Pelton:
- Clan Falconer's War
- The Rise of the Rebellion
- Changeling's Clan

Other Authors with Potpourri Publishing

Lynette Spencer

- Basic Sewing on a Budget
- Vegetarian Cooking on a Budget

Dan Pelton

- The Majestic Spectrum of God's Love

Dedication

First to God, who is ever my protector and source of creativity.

To all my Christian brothers and sisters, may we all meet on the east side of the Tree of Life, third Sabbath into our life in heaven and find out just where all our journeys led us after reading this book. I can't wait to meet you all.

To my family, Dan, my long suffering husband and the only person who could have put up with me for over half my life; Fawn/Scott, Miah/Tiff/Malachi/Lukas, Ben/Beni, Alana, Tris, my children, grandchildren and loved ones, thank you for not thinking you have the absolutely craziest mom/grandma in the universe as I worked on this book and muttered the incantations of Scripture and famous men's thoughts in an effort to find just the right words to say what I was being led to say.

Next, to my parents and my sister who walked the Red Road before me, and who I will see again someday in the Skylands. I miss you every day.

Finally, to my readers, because a story isn't a story until someone else hears it; it is simply a phantasm, a dream in the maker's head. You make it live when you read it. I hope the vision put in my head by He Who Creates with a Thought enters your soul as well as you read these poor words, and you walk ever closer to Him.

Table of Contents

Introduction

Beginning the Steps to a New Habit

<u>Gifted Thoughts</u>

<u>Story Number</u>
1	2 Corinthians 4:17
2	1 Corinthians 12:1,4
3	Acts 13:47
4	Romans 12:10
5	Luke 12:15
6	Matthew 6:14
7	I Thessalonians 4:16-17
8	1 Corinthians 4:2
9	1 John 2:10
10	Psalms 23:6
11	Proverbs 25:11
12	Genesis 1:26
13	Psalms 91:11
14	2 Peter 3:18
15	1 John 4:18
16	Matthew 12:36
17	1 Peter 5:7
18	Romans 12:3
19	Romans 12:10
20	1 Corinthians 10:13
21	Exodus 14:13
22	Isaiah 62:2
23	Romans 1:16
24	1 Peter 3:15

Congratulations

25	James 1:26
26	Psalms 58:3
27	1 John 4:10
28	Romans 10:9,10
29	I Corinthians 10:13
30	Proverbs 3:1-35, selected phrases
31	John 3:16, 17
32	James 4:7
33	Hebrews 13:1-3
34	John 14:6
35	1 Timothy 6:6-10
36	Philippians 4:8-9
37	James 2:14-24
38	1 Corinthians 13:1-13
39	1 John 1:9
40	John 16:33
41	Ezekiel 34:26
42	1 Peter 5:5
43	Isaiah 55:11
44	Proverbs 6:20
45	Ephesians 2:8,9
46	Genesis 3:6

People to Help You Maintain Change

47	Isaiah 26:3-4
48	John 16:33
49	Isaiah 41:10
50	Proverbs 16:7
51	Proverbs 22:29
52	John 16:22
53	Psalms 118:24

54	1 Corinthians 12:7
55	James 1:5
56	John 12:26
57	Matthew 6-25-34
58	1 Timothy 4:12
59	2 Timothy 1:7
60	Luke 11:13

Things That Have Shaped Me

61	1 Peter 5:7
62	Philippians 4:6-7
63	Isaiah 41:10
64	Isaiah 46:4
65	Deuteronomy 31:6
66	Psalms 118:6
67	Romans 6:28
68	Psalms 11:1-16
69	Isaiah 54:17
70	Habakkuk 3:17-19
71	Psalms 46:1
72	2 Corinthians 5:17
73	Psalm 119:165
74	Joel 2:12-13
75	Psalm 34:18
76	2 Chronicles 7:14

Stories to Change Your Worldview

77	John 17:3
78	Galatians 6:10
79	Jeremiah 29:11
80	Psalms 79:12
81	Psalms 32:5
82	Psalms 118:24
83	Isaiah 29:18

84	2 Corinthians 5:17
85	James 1:22-27
86	Revelation 21:10,21:1,3,4
87	Romans 1:16-17
88	John 16:33
89	Romans 8:6
90	John 12:26

A Final Word
Promised Book Suggestions
My Prayer Requests Pages
Free Story
Short Autobiography
A Request
A Free Chapter
Bibliography of Journal Articles
Smiling

Introduction

Curiosity and the Spirit made you pick up this book: the idea of escaping a hum-drum, inadequate form of spirituality has intrigued that part of you that still has hope; the normality of having a commonplace experience instead of what God intended gnaws at the edge of your mind. If you are reading this book, I am assuming the idea of getting closer to God in just a few short weeks has intrigued you, whetted your appetite and touched your soul. You may be a searcher, or someone dissatisfied with a lukewarm state of soul or you may be someone who has long walked with Him and feel that for some reason nothing is working anymore. You feel as if the prayer warrior within you has gone on vacation and shows no sign of coming back from the beach.

At any rate, you have tried and failed to set up anything that has worked for long to bring you closer to God and the peace of mind that brings. You are tired of halfway change. Your Christianity has turned into yearly resolutions that are kept about as well as sudden diets. You may think the routine of daily life does not allow you time to bring yourself in sync with God; there are not enough hours in the day to pray and study; keep up with everything leaves you feeling dissatisfied and upset. Whatever the reason, you are looking for some way, some reason, some formula or schematic or equation to make the unease go away. I felt that way once and what I learned about escaping that feeling is the rationale behind this book. I have hope for you, based on my own experience, solid provable research into how your mind works and a faith that this is what God wants me to write for you. I was where you are once. I found a way out, and I want you to come along the constantly narrowing path to God-achievers.

Among the roles I fill in my life are Wife, Mother, Grandmother, church planter, shepherd, farmer, author, artist and Social Worker. The ways people live their lives fascinates me. I never have quite enough time to read all the journal studies done about people. I do try, although sometimes I find it's hard to comb through all the jargon to find small nuggets of truth that I find useful in my work in counseling and coaching people. Over the years, the gleaning and application of what I learn while doing private study to what people who come to me need is a cause and effect sort of serendipity not unlike a choir or music group playing; you know it works, but unless you're the orchestra conductor or the composer you are never quite sure how it goes together, it simply does and it makes the listening a pleasure. The aha! moments I see in my office as something clicks within people is a wonder I don't get over. I like to see it happen so I keep track of what seems to be the most problematic for my patients and for my church members and then I go into research mode to find answers for them and in doing so, often find it helps me as well. In the last few years of work, I have noticed people are frustrated by mediocrity; they are tired of the sameness, they want something to pull them to a safer shore, but a shore where there is creativity and kindness, love and no loneliness, a place of acceptance and energy.

They want to make changes, especially within their spiritual lives, but the habit of get up, eat, work, home again, shower, TV/social media and sleep, over and over, is killing them. The habits of a drone like existence makes them lonely, angry, bitter and helpless. Since we weren't designed to be hermits, nor to run along a hamster trail, it's no wonder our habits are destroying our lives.

A short while back, I got very interested in habits; habits being automatic behaviors that have been wired into our brains through repetition; I wanted to find out what it takes to make them, what it takes to break them, how we can control them. Too many of the people I work with were struggling with stopping the consequences of habits they'd made early in life and now were paying for, yet felt helpless to do anything. Their habits were killing them. They'd developed them early in life and they wanted them to go away. They wouldn't go easily without a struggle and the struggle is what we need to make stop. You can't get rid of consequences, they happen as cause and effect. For instance, you smoke two packs a day for twenty years, you will most likely develop lung cancer or some form of lung disease. Will stopping smoking stop the disease? No, of course not. It will help you get stronger, but you will still have to fight the cancer battle which your own actions caused to occur.

It's a little like taming lions. When a lion is little, (or so I am told. I do not raise lions, only children, alpaca, Pomeranians, canaries and Siamese cats) when a lion is less than three months old, they are cuddly and easy to play with and they are simple to get away from. You stand up, slip them off your lap and walk away. They may give chase but they really aren't all that hurtful. When a lion grows larger, say nine months, they are much more determined, stronger, and it might take someone helping you, interceding as it were, to get away from a determined young lion. You'll come away with bites, scratches and a decided decision not to go in that cage again. But once a lion is full grown, you need someone with a gun or a tranquilizer dart to slow it down or kill it outright and you will not get out unscathed. You will get hurt. You could even die. The same is true for habits. You can smoke a cigarette or a joint once or twice with friends and put it down. You can overindulge on alcohol, or tell white lies, or cheat on your taxes and probably get away with it for a time. You can neglect to pray daily, and think to come back to it. As time goes on, and you continue to smoke, the poisons that are addictive get stronger and harder to overcome. You can still stop doing it, but you may need some help, like nicotine patches, a support group or a good scare from your doctor. As time goes on, not praying, not actively putting God first will gradually lead to a sort of spiritual ennui that is much like Alzheimer's-you remember things in the past but the present state of your soul eludes you. The Spirit wants to talk to you, and sometimes you rouse yourself enough to go to a revival meeting for a few days, but after the hype is over, you slip and nothing changes except the load of guilt you feel.

If you have neglected God for some time, you are going to need to put some effort into getting back into His throne room, feeling comfortable with His presence again. Do not think I am saying He has left you; no, but just as any other earthly friend, you can drift apart and the first steps back into friendship feel awkward; after asking about the job, and the kids and the weather, what do you talk about? You can restart your spiritual life, you can regain the place you once held in His presence and feel His help, but you may need some prodding from someone who loves you. He knew that and He sent us his Holy Spirit to get us to remember just when we need it. (John 14:26 But the Helper, the Holy Spirit, whom the Father will send in My name, He will teach you all things, and bring to your remembrance all things that I said to you.)

I know from experience, the longer you let it wait, put it aside, and think I'll do it tonight, or tomorrow morning, or when Lent comes or it's going to be my New Years' resolution next year, you come to the place where it seems too hard, there are simply too many distractions to read the Bible, or think of Him, or talk to Him. You have officially drifted and eventually that Old Serpent will whisper you've gone too far, it's too hard, you're too busy, nobody does that anymore and you wander into a complacent mode. You know you're a Christian although you can't quite remember to call on Him when needed, or where that verse in the Bible was that you need right now, and your soul somewhat closes its' spiritual eyes and goes to sleep. The Spirit, in an attempt to wake you up, sometimes resorts to extreme measures to get your attention, and sometimes, even that doesn't work anymore. Has God moved? No, you lost anchor, you are out to sea and you need rescued. When it gets that far, you need a complete revival, a re-doing of your habits, a turning back, repentance if you will, in order to regain that first love, that flush of affection, that security that He is there for you. It's not something to day dream about or reminisce about, it's a call to action. Sometimes something out of the ordinary comes along and you suddenly realize you've neglected Him so much you're afraid to talk to Him. The cancer comes or the car wreck happens, or the marriage problems start, you lose your job, whatever the crisis may be, and you find yourself lost with no one to comfort you and you wonder where is God? He didn't go anywhere. You wandered. The fact that you have gotten a copy of this book may be a leading of the Spirit to bring you back to Him. This book is written to help you find your straight path out of the bad habit of ignoring the Lord of the Universe and engaging in behavior that will being you closer to heaven. This book will help you develop a habit of putting God first and accepting His leading and His rewards.

So if you're trying to get back to Him, or perhaps you never knew Him in the first place, or perhaps you're a new believer and wanted to make changes in the right way, whichever is the case, let me assure you, He is a gentleman, He is a lover, He is still there waiting for you to make an appointment with Him every day. The question you ask me is simple: how do I get from point A-which is where I am- to point B, where I want to be, in the shortest, fastest way possible? I am glad you asked. With a prayer and a song, let's begin our odyssey, the pilgrimage we are beginning to activate our God Habit.

Beginning the Steps to a New Habit

The first step to change a habit is to admit you want and need to actually change that habit. You must decide to take action. Picking up this book and reading it day by day is one action. Setting an actual appointment to meet with God is another action. Setting aside the things blocking your carry through are a third. But let's look at the process of change itself.

Research has shown us it takes 24 days to change a habit, to extinguish it, 24 days of not doing what you always did, in this case, your habit of neglecting to meet with God. (In the end matter, I have listed some pertinent journal articles that may help understand this better: there are literally hundreds of them out there but I found these most helpful.) But how do we actually accomplish a new habit?

You first decide a habit needs to change, you feel an inner compulsion that this is the right thing to do. You pre-contemplate it at first, think yes, that's a good idea, maybe this book will help; if it doesn't help it actually wouldn't hurt, do I want to do this? Yes, I do. The Spirit is involved in this, as He is always in matters of the children of the King, waiting patiently for you to catch up. You make a decision finally, so you pick up the book, find a place to sit down and begin to read; you have contemplated change and you are now taking actions, steps to do it.

You find that the next step is to make a daily appointment, a commitment to meet with God. This is another step along the trip. You have decided, made the choice to make change happen, and you are now actively involved in doing that. Have we got a new habit yet? No, but we're in process of change. (I suspect your guardian angel is cheering you on at this point.)

To make the appointment with God happen, it helps to have a schedule. You schedule everything else, job at 9 to 5 or 3 to 11, Monday through Friday, sometimes overtime, right? You schedule dental appointments and dates to get together with friends, doctor appointments and play dates for the kids. Why is your appointment to God any different? Schedules build habits. In my research of the topic, I found that science has shown us it takes 24 days to break a habit, 66 days to build a habit. So in this book, we take ninety days to help you build a habit of daily meeting with Him; growing in His love and learning to depend on His care.

Any trip, voyage, pilgrimage begins with preparation. This is no different. You need to commit yourself each day to taking fifteen minutes and putting it in your day planner as a regular appointment with Him, just like all your other appointments for the day. You need to make it an unbreakable appointment, even if the alarm doesn't go off when expected, or the boss is pushy or life sends you other deadlines - because life will seem to send crisis as soon as you try to move closer to God. It just seems to happen. You need to set your fifteen minutes in a safe, quiet space. I know of one woman who uses her commute from Boston to New York each day on the train as her time. I know another who gets up half an hour earlier than needed for work, slips out of the bedroom to avoid waking her mate and locks herself in the downstairs bathroom. Another person I know is a farmer; he goes out to care for the animals and sits in his hay loft to talk to God. I have a friend who goes out to his RV, slips in and sits in the back; he leaves his book and prayer list there on the RV table and each day slips out at lunchtime, closes the door and I'm not sure if his family has realized it or not, but it's become a sacred place to him. You need to find your place and your time. I prefer morning because throughout the day, I think back to what I've read and what He directed me to think about. If you find that sometime doing a lunch hour makes sense, then do it then. I have found just before bed to be more difficult because we all have a tendency to fall asleep when tired and it's harder to learn new things when tired. It is entirely up to you: God makes appointments 24 hours a day. His book is open and waiting for your appointment.

Once you have set your appointment, set this book where you will see it. Don't hide it. Put it on your bedside stand where it's there in the morning when you get up. Have a pen with it. If you are doing it at lunch at work, then put it where you will have it at hand. I've tried to make the cover bright enough to not miss easily. Put it where you will be studying, but not out of sight.

Now, take a post it note or two. Write on them: remember my appointment at (fill in this spot). No one needs to know what the appointment is but you and Him. No one questions appointment reminders stuck on calendars or in day planners or on the fridge. So, stick it on the fridge, on the bathroom cabinet mirror, wherever you think you need to put one to remind you. You have no idea how good the devil is at preventing you from starting to go anywhere near God.

So it's 6:00 a.m. or noon or whenever you've set for this task. Turn off your phone. Pick up the book. The book is your cue to your appointment. Sit in a comfortable position and turn to the right page. The journey starts now. Are you excited yet? You ought to be. The changes you make over the next few weeks are going to be life changing. Each day of this journey, you will first request He meet with you as you are reading and considering the day's reading. Close your eyes and say something like:

Heavenly Father, I'm here for our appointment., Help me to learn a little bit more today than I knew before. Don't let anything interrupt us. I am trying to learn to love you more. In Jesus's name, Amen.

Open your eyes and read the story for the day. They aren't long and won't take more than a couple minutes. Think about the Scripture quoted, and the quote at the bottom and how they may have something for you to consider.

After you have completed reading, take a moment next and think first of a blessing you have been given and write it down. It might be hearing the birds outside your window singing. It might be someone's new baby; something good that happened at work, a flowering bush you passed while taking your morning walk or jog, or just waking up not feeling rushed. It's as simple or it's as complex as you want it to be, but write it down.

Next you think of a family member, a friend, or a need of your own, and write it down. Finally, you ask Him for His care and guidance throughout the day. These are the outline of your prayer. I have put a form at the bottom of the reading each day for the first 24 days for you. You probably won't need that long to remember how to do it, but fill it out, close your eyes and talk to God. We'll explain what to do after the first part of setting up your God habit is completed. (Remember it takes 24 days to change the habit of not meeting with God each day; so at the end of day 24, we celebrate and start replacing the old bad habit of ignoring God with the new good one of meeting with Him.) For the first twenty-four days, follow the outline in your prayer of praise, thanks, request and closing. Your outline will look like something like this and the prayer somewhat the same:

Heavenly Father, I praise you for (whatever it is you want to praise him about-be it the earth, your friends/family, the lovely robins heralding spring, whatever you want to Praise him about.)

I am thankful today for

_____

–

(Thank you God for is another way to say it)

Please help

_____

_(need of your own, person you want God to help; just one or two, not a laundry list.)

Give me this day to walk closer to you, to serve others and to learn all that I need to know to be your child again. In thy Son's name, Amen

So the closing prayer you say will be individual to you but can sound something like:

"Heavenly Father, Praise you for your wonders, the earth, the sky, the sea and all that lives within them.
   Thank you for my family, my friends and my pets.
   Please help my husband this day and lead him to be the man you want him to be.
   Give me this day to walk closer to you, to serve others and to learn all that I need to know to be your child again. In thy Son's name, Amen"

All of this together should take no longer than fifteen minutes, but you may find after you've been journeying for a while, you find yourself praying longer and wishing for more time; that's pretty normal. I remember a story about the Reformation leader Martin Luther. One day, he was talking to his wife Catherine and he stated, "I am going to be so busy today, I simply must pray for at least three hours before I begin." I don't expect that of you to start and you shouldn't be frustrated if you don't go into a mystical trance or become an instant prayer warrior. However, as you get closer to Him, the time goes quickly in His presence. I just thought I'd better warn you.

That's all there is to making this habit: but you must do it every day for it to work to best efficiency. Don't get in the habit of doing it a couple times, or try it for a week and then get distracted. There are going to be all sorts of things to try and stop you; persevere. The importance of why we do this just this way is simple and scientific and really quite elegant.

Your brain is a wondrous machine. Neuroscientists have found that there is a part of our brain called the basal ganglia that is involved in making habits. A habit forms a neural pathway in the brain. Once a neural pathway for a habit is established, it never really goes away. It can be altered which is what we are doing. There is a pattern to forming habits: there is something that triggers a behavior, scientists call that a cue. There is a reaction to that cue. If the action ends up feeling good, or rewarding you, you will repeat the action when you see the cue again. This forms a neural path.

Seeing the book on your bedside stand or your lunchbox will trigger the cue and you reach automatically after a while for your reading and by the time you get to the 80th day, you'll wonder what to do next, and I have a list of books at the end, most by writers I have never met but have gained much from, who could help you along the path: and I have suggestions of Bible passages you could also use to continue your journey.

If you make habit of setting your mind to God, your brain will makes pathways that lead you closer to Him. He made you that way. Visiting with Him daily becomes a behavior, a set point in your life, to think of Him and His thoughts. Ninety days may seem a long time in this era of rushing about. However, I can assure you that the journey towards Him is never long; He is there with His arms stretched wide to receive you, to sit down and share a cup of coffee, to sympathize and breathe life into your soul.

The travel is not without risks and not without work, but it is rewarding in ways you cannot see right now. I am honored to be your guide for the next three months: three months that may just change everything you thought you knew about His care and leading.

Daily time with Him will aid you in staying closer to the One who loves you. Can a marriage stay intact without communication? If a parent never talks to their child, will that child respect them? Daily time with Him, getting in touch with God, will help you make better choices in your life, and it will help you to accept the simple promptings of the Spirit. You will become one of His own. God bless you as you begin this trip towards heaven and home. Are you ready? Have you got a pen or pencil? Then turn the page and let's begin with day 1!

March 24th 2020

We have small troubles for a while now, but they are helping us gain an enternal glory that is much greater than the troubles.

Day One

Heavenly Father, I'm here for our appointment., Help me to learn a little bit more today than I knew before. Don't let anything interrupt us. I am trying to love you more. In Jesus's name, Amen.

2nd Corinthians 4:17
For our light affliction, which is but for a moment works for us a far more exceeding weight of glory.

What do Babe Ruth, Ty Cobb, Charlie Chaplin, Michelangelo, Ross Perot, George Bush, Bill Clinton, Jack the Ripper and Napoleon all have in common? Give up? They were all left-handed or 'sinstrol factoids' in scientific terms. Did that prevent them from being successful? Did God love them any less?

Lefties have always been looked at as a little odd. Only one in ten humans are left-handed. One in 10 struggles with scissors built wrong, and clothes that button on the wrong side and all the appliances of life built backwards to what they need. Everything is made for the right-handers. It used to be believed that lefties were witches and had made a pact with the devil. After all, hadn't Christ said in chapter 25 of Matthew, "then shall He say on to them on the left hand, depart from me, ye cursed, into everlasting fire, prepared for the Devils and his angels?" Back in the Middle Ages, you could get burned at the stake for using the "wrong" hand.

So, okay, you say, that was all superstition. That's all behind us now, isn't it? Having spoken to a few lefties, I wonder sometimes. Even in the languages we speak, the world is against lefties. The word left in English comes from the Anglo-Saxon word *lyft*, which means weak or broken. Gauche in French means left, it also means uncouth. Link is left in German, it also means awkward. In Spanish izquierdo means left, and crooked. If you are left-handed in Russian, Nnalyevo; you are also a black marketer. So what's a lefty to do?

You could move to Left Hand, West Virginia, population 600. You could join Left-handers International. I kid you not, this organization offers help for lefties. They have a catalog of properly oriented objects, scissors to can openers, that makes life a lot easier if you're left-handed. They also have sponsored August 13 as Left-handers Day. They fight for the rights of the directionally challenged.

Why am I bringing this up at the start of our trip? We need to think about preconceived ideas. God made all sorts of people; He loves diversity; He loves our quirks, our eccentricities, our different sizes and shapes and colors. We as Christians need to know that God loves all people, right or left-handed. It is irrelevant to God just as color, size and shape are irrelevant to Him. He loves us, just as we are.

There used to be a grand gentleman called Mr. Rogers who had a Neighborhood. At the end of each segment of the program, he almost always said , "You always make the day special. Do you know how? By just your being you. I like you just the way you are." God is like that. He is welcoming, He likes you for yourself.

You could pray for the tolerance to love everyone, not just the un-different ones. If we all prayed for tolerance of each other, what might happen to this world?

Incidentally, next time you see a picture of the Sistine Chapel, notice God is touching Adam on his left hand to give him life; God also put your heart on the left side of your body. The Hebrews and the Arabs write right to left. Boy Scouts shake hands with their left hands; The Incas thought left-handers were capable of healing and that they possessed magical abilities. The North American Zuni tribe believed left-handedness signified good luck; and finally tests conducted by St. Lawrence University in New York found that there were more left-handed people with IQs over 140 than right-handed people. I could go on, but I think you see: Infinite Diversity in Infinite Combinations isn't just in science fiction; it's in life. As His children, <u>we need to accept others in all their wonderful differences, and love all people and respect them just as He did when He designed them.</u>

"The Christian life is not slightly better, but completely different."

Clarence Sexton

Heavenly Father, I praise you for

for the rain outside + the thunder

I am thankful today for
Parker + Kennedy being at my house +
not bothering me as I read this chapter

Please help
Dana + help me Love her as you do
help me see her through your eyes

Give me this day to walk closer to you, to serve others and to learn all that I need to know to be your child again. In thy Son's name, Amen

Now on to your day to walk with Him!

Thank you Jesus

March 25 2020
There are different kinds of gifts but they are all from the same Spirit

Day Two

Heavenly Father, I'm here for our appointment., Help me to learn a little bit more today than I knew before. Don't let anything interrupt us. I am trying to love you more. In Jesus's name, Amen.

1 Corinthians 12:1, 4
"Now concerning spiritual gifts, brethren, I do not want you to be ignorant . . . There are diversities of gifts, but the same Spirit."

There once was a man called Luigi Tarisio. He collected violins. And when I say that, I mean he *collected* violins! When he died, in his home were found 246 exquisite instruments, which he had been collecting for years – all collecting dust in boxes and bureau drawers. In his devotion to the instrument, he had prevented the world from hearing the music from the instruments he collected.

A violin is useless unless it's played. It might as well be plywood and cellophane if it isn't used. Luigi robbed the world and he robbed himself, for in his mania for violins, he made himself a pauper. He had many thousands of dollars' worth of violins, and he died hungry and sick and cold and lonely.

Can it be that we are like that sometimes? We are so afraid someone won't appreciate our talents that we don't use them at all. We act like misers. Both us and the world suffers.

So you don't sing like Sandy Patti and you don't have rhythm like Michael W. Smith and you can't play and write music like Gershwin and you don't have money like Trump or Gates – who cares? You're you. That's important to God and to the ones you care about you. You've got talents. You've got gifts. You need to acknowledge what they are and discover how to use them.

My husband and I took a spiritual gifts seminar at our local church. I found out I'm a helper and a prayer warrior. Dan has the gift of martyrdom. (Does that explain why we've been married so long?) It makes me a little nervous when I think of the last days and the tribulation as preached by some pastors and the actual end of all things. However, Dan also has other gifts he uses for God, like music and empathy and leadership.

Maybe you aren't a leader. We aren't all leaders. There's a place for enthusiastic followers, too. Maybe you have the gift of helps; I think it's the most important gift given to the church and the most needed. We can't always use the teacher or preacher, but everybody needs a helper for something.

Think of what you are good at, what you love doing. It could be gardening; it could be bread making or maybe you're one of those athletic types who run a lot. Think of your interactions with other people. Are you better in crowds or behind the scenes. Do you l ike the up front of teaching or would you rather make the potluck run. Then consider how God could use that gift in service-and potluck runners may end up helping in free meals for the poor, and athletic kinds could end up coaching little league and being an example of great sportsmanship.

So don't just sit there. Find out your gift and give it back to God in service. He loaned it to you to invest in Him. Make your life a wise investment.

> "We do not become righteous by doing righteous deeds but, having been made righteous, we do righteous deeds."
>
> Martin Luther

Heavenly Father, I praise you for _Letting me sing & play the Guitar_

I am thankful today for _being able to go to work_

Please help _Barbara, Pat & Rod, Faye_

Give me this day to walk closer to you, to serve others and to learn all that I need to know to be your child again. In thy Son's name, Amen

March 26 2026

I have made you a light for the nations you will show people all over the world the way to be saved

Day Three

Heavenly Father, I'm here for our appointment., Help me to learn a little bit more today than I knew before. Don't let anything interrupt us. I am trying to love you more. In Jesus's name, Amen.

Acts 13:47
"For so the Lord has commanded us: 'I have set you as a light to the Gentiles,
That you should be for salvation to the ends of the earth."

Without light, you can't see anything. No light equals very dark; for instance like a cave or a mine or a basement without windows. That's simple enough, even toddlers know this and want a nightlight. What is light made of? Scientists tells us it's made of waves or particles -there's a disagreement on that- but they all agree it has frequency, and the different frequencies, when seen by our eyes, make all the colors in our world.

White light is made up of all colors: together they are called a spectrum. Without all the colors you don't have white light. That's just science. Have you thought about light lately? Have you looked through a prism and seen light broken down into its parts? When you last saw a rainbow, did you wonder what the colors might mean?

I wanted to find out other things about light so I decided to look up and find out what symbolism the colors might have. Let me tell you about the meanings of the colors you see every day.

White is the symbol of pure love. God is pure love. He is love incarnate. He contains everything and is everything. All the colors combine and make white light.

Red is the color of blood and symbolizes passion and security and it has the longest wavelength. God had so much passion in trying to give us the security of a future home, he shed his blood and died. He is longsuffering towards us and forgiving.

Orange is a combination of yellow and red and represents creativity, playfulness and control; God is in control, he loves to create and He loves us to be creative. And playful? Really? Have you looked at a duck-billed platypus or a possum carrying it's babies on its back, keeping them in a pouch? He could have made the animal kingdom all dogs, or all cats but He wanted us to have the joy of watching baby goats spronging around. He wanted us to watch dolphins and listen to birds and see sunsets. God is the epitome of creativity.

Yellow is the color of patience and wisdom.. Like gold, patience is precious. Sunshine is yellow; so are a lot of the flowers in spring that we wait so long to see, daffodils, crocus and forsythia. Wisdom, a word spoken at the right time to the right person, is like apples of gold in pictures of silver.

Green is the symbol of mercy, growth and health. God is all merciful. All over the planet to remind us of mercy, He made green living things and eating our greens makes us healthy. As long as a plant has green in it, it will live. God originally placed us in a garden to be gardeners and care for this earth as good stewards. He is still interested in our environment.

Blue is the color of loyalty and law. In ancient days, the Jews wore a blue ribbon around the hems of their garments to represent their loyalty to God and His law of liberty. The United States flag has a back color of blue for loyalty.

Purple is the color of royalty and of sorrow. God is the royalty of our universe. He is the Lord of all the worlds. His sorrow over our sins caused Him to send His Son as the Man of sorrows, despised, rejected and acquainted with grief. He feels our grief, He knows the pain and He comforts us. His purple bruises paid for our sins.

If you add all colors together in light, you get white, the symbol of purity and love. If you see a rainbow from an airplane overhead, it's actually a circle. We normally here on earth only see half of it. Only from up above can you see all the circle at once. That's a symbol of the totality, the wholeness of God and His creation. When you see a rainbow, think of the attributes of God. If you read the final two chapters of Revelation, the last book of the Bible, the description of the holy city tells us that its' foundation stones are all jewels, precious stones, layer upon layer. From outside the city, looking at it, the pure light of God will shine through the jewels, refracting the light into bands of bright shining colors. What an amazing thing to see! And remember, you can be there someday.

Next time you see our half of the rainbow, think of our home to come. And think of the wholeness of God.

"Don't seek to be happy; let everyone else chase after that rainbow. Seek to be kind, and you'll find the rainbow follows you.".

Richelle E. Goodrich

Heavenly Father, I praise you for
new life in all the trees budding + flowers coming to bloom

I am thankful today for
My family + friends. That you are shutting down the Corno virus

Please help
me today Lord I'm struggling all who are sick

Give me this day to walk closer to you, to serve others and to learn all that I need to know to be your child again. Thank you for color. In thy Son's name, Amen

March 27 2020

Love each other like brothers & sisters. Give each other more honor than you want for yourselves

Day Four

Heavenly Father, I'm here for our appointment., Help me to learn a little bit more today than I knew before. Don't let anything interrupt us. I am trying to love you more. In Jesus's name, Amen.

Romans 12:10
Love one another with brotherly affection. Outdo one another in showing honor.

I have raised six children. At this writing they're all adults. Some of them have their own kids now and I have the sweetest grandchildren in the whole world (ok, I am a bit prejudiced; show me a grandma who isn't.) But I remember when they were small. I remember when they were clingy little toddlers wanting so much to explore the world and wanting to be sure mother was close by while they did the exploring. We used to go on business trips with their dad. I think we've been to every zoo in the Midwest, many of the museums, and most parks and public playgrounds. We homeschooled and all the trips were field trips. To this day, they all love zoos and museums.

I well remember how wide-eyed they would get looking at the animals. All of them stayed with me usually except for Emily. You see, Emily had curiosity that was phenomenal and it matched her personality as well. She still can't wait to see what's around the next corner. On our trips, she'd get curious and next thing I knew, she'd wander off. Then Ben would follow her, and Fawn would go looking to find the lost ones, and Miah would start crying. It got so bad I finally got harnesses for all 4 of them. One week after we got the harnesses we were at the Ohio State fair. It was the biggest in the country at that time. I was congratulating myself on my good sense when I saw mini cam filming us. I didn't think too much about it as it appeared to be filming the fair more than us. Then I got home and the phone calls started. You see, the mini cam came from the TV station, not our local one, the big one from Columbus. All over the state of Ohio, I was the lady in the crowd with the 4 little kids on the leashes all of them going off in different directions, while I pulled wagon with our gear behind us, sort of a reverse chariot. I felt like a child abuser caught in the act. There was no way I could explain to the thousands of people who saw me I was doing it for their own good. Oh, I was so frustrated. And come church that week, the number of folks who saw us on the 6:00 news was stunning. I had no idea so many watched channel 10.

    I imagine God has the same problem. The whole universe is watching over one small planet to see what will happen in the war between good and evil. To protect us from danger, He has to give some rules that may not make sense sometimes to us or the surrounding universe. He hopes we will understand. He must feel like a bully sometimes when we fuss about the rules. But the rules are there to keep us safe. And if we could understand what was behind the rules, we would have made them the same way. Just like the leashes and halters, when the kids were old enough, I no longer had to use them. They understand now why I used them back then and they laugh about it. At the time they really didn't like them because it interrupted their adventures.

In the same way, God really loves us and He knows what is best. Let's trust him and his judgment and keep the rules He has set up for us to live by. His barriers, His boundaries are safety nets for us here. <u>Someday we'll understand His concern and His caring as he reins us in before we get hurt.</u>

"I like your Christ, I do not like your Christians. Your Christians are so unlike your Christ."
                        Mahatma Gandhi

Heavenly Father, I praise you for *your word, the sunshine, new life rules*

I am thankful today for *That my knee is better! Warm weather. Your safety nets that surround me!*

Please help *Stacy, Dana, Seth, Daley, + Lesley, Bradley, Chris, Melissa, Austin, Scott.*

Give me this day to walk closer to you, to serve others and to learn all that I need to know to be your child again. Thank you for your safety net keeping me secure. In thy Son's name, Amen

[Handwritten at top: March 28th 2020 off work till April 17 for corona virus]

[Handwritten above title: Then Jesus said to them, Be careful + guard against (your heart) all Kinds of Greed. Life is not measured by how much one owns.]

Day Five

Heavenly Father, I'm here for our appointment., Help me to learn a little bit more today than I knew before. Don't let anything interrupt us. I am trying to love you more. In Jesus's name, Amen.

Luke 12:15
Take heed and beware of covetousness for man's life consists not in the abundance of things he possesses.

Have you ever held a hamster? These cute furry beasties are one of my favorite pocket pets. They are small enough that even someone in an apartment can have one without fearing any damage to the apartment. Hamsters are nocturnal. They are active at night. They spend much of their day curled into a ball in the corner. They do not like to be woke up by anybody, and they can nip you if you wake them up. And you know what the oddest thing is about these little guys? It's their cheeks. Hands down, their cheeks are their biggest talent.

Hamsters hoard food, especially seeds. They have cheek pouches and will stuff those pouches full of food; scramble around to a corner and empty their pouches into it; cover the stash and then run back to their food dish for another load. They do eat some of it, of course, but most of what you give them will be found secreted in corners. It doesn't matter that you're faithful to feed them every day.

They still hoard it. This is what makes them such a danger in their homeland of Russia and Asia. They will steal grain from farmers' fields in such great quantities that they endanger the people living there. They have found hamster nests with as much is 6 bushels of grain stored in them! And the rodents multiply so rapidly that even with lots of traps and cats they are huge problem.

Now if we were in danger of famine, I could almost understand the need to hoard food. In the Bible, in the Old testament stories, there was a man named Joseph who convinced Pharaoh to lay up food in good times because seven years of famine were coming. Due to Pharaoh listening, not only Egypt but all the lands around it were saved from starvation. Some folks today feel that we will someday have a big interruption in the food chain and they put up survival rations. That's well and good and might even be prudent in some instances. That is not what this little story we're reading about in today's journey is about.

The hamster reminds me of some people I know. They have much more than they'll ever need to live on and yet they're always looking to find ways to get more; to build up savings accounts or to own more stock; to have three cars or four, to have the latest and greatest of everything. They are seemingly never satisfied. I am sorry to say some Christians are that way, too. They have never learned that the riches of heaven, their blessings on earth and talents from God are worthless if they do nothing with them. They won't sing at church, they won't play piano for junior church, they haven't got time to visit the lonely or elderly and they surely don't have any extra money for a special offering for missions! Just like the little hamster they go through life hoarding their blessings, running on their hamster wheel, never sharing, allowing their selfishness to grow. Are they busy? Oh, yes. Are they happy? Not really. Only people who give are ever really happy. It's one of God's spiritual laws. If you give, you have more to give, and you feel good about it. Smiling at others gains you smiles in return, doing random acts of kindness makes you simply feel good. It's God's way; after all, isn't He the one who invented kindness?

"You can't have a perfect day without doing something for someone who'll never be able to repay you."
John Wooden

Heavenly Father, I praise you for _helping me to be less selfish. I'm not there yet, but with your help I'm getting there_

I am thankful today for _for the blessing I received at work from people giving me extra money_

Please help _me know to do what you would do about paying the rent._

Give me this day to walk closer to you, to serve others and to learn all that I need to know to be your child again. Help me to find someone to be kind to today. In thy Son's name, Amen

March 24, 2020

Yes, if you forgive others for their sins, your Father in heaven will also forgive you for your sins

Day Six

Heavenly Father, I'm here for our appointment., Help me to learn a little bit more today than I knew before. Don't let anything interrupt us. I am trying to love you more. In Jesus's name, Amen.

Matthew 6:14 for if ye forgive men their trespasses, your heavenly father will also forgive you.

When my brother was a boy he had a raccoon named Calamity Jane, mostly because of her insatiable curiosity. It got her into so much trouble! Once she figured out how to open the door to her pen she would go off to explore, then hustle back if she thought she'd been caught, slam the door shut and get busy with her water bowl. One time, we caught her washing rocks in her bowl, acting terribly interested. Looking around, we found she'd been harassing the bantam hens in their pen.

Another time she got in the kitchen and smelled something tasty so she ended up on the table where she discovered a bowl of bread dough. Oh, how much fun! You could push it and knead it and taste it occasionally. She ended up dumping it on the floor right along with the bag of flour. She heard mom, and ran out across the carpeting, leaving little white prints all over the green carpet, hustling back into her cage. Now in those days, my mom made big batches of bread, 7 or 8 loaves at a time and she was none too pleased to see the day's work on the floor. She made my brother clean it up. And dad put a lock on the door where CJ couldn't reach it.

One of CJ's favorite pranks was called drown the cat. (At least I think that's what she would've called it if she could talk). We had this big old long-haired tomcat named Sinbad. He loved to relax in the sun on a stump near the pond. CJ would watch until Sinbad was nice and quiet and sneak up to yank his tail. Sinbad would shriek and run for the nearest tree which had this long limb over the pond. CJ would chase him up the tree and onto that branch, then ease out after him. The combined weight would bend the branch and they'd both fall in the pond. Now the dunking didn't bother the coon but oh, the cat! Such a yowling he would set up until mom came to rescue him.

My brother used to put CJ on a leash and take CJ for walks around town. He'd ride my brother's shoulder. He'd bring along a pocket full of treats and let other kids feed the coon. Everybody in the neighborhood loved CJ. except one guy who was a hunter.

You see back then coon pelts were worth $35 each. This guy knew CJ was tame and would be an easy catch so one night after we'd gone to bed, he brought some treats, got her out of the cage, hit her on the head and skinned her. My brother found her body the next day and when he got to school, he was told who did it since the guy had been bragging about how easy his latest kill had been and was flashing the money he'd made for the pelt. My little brother is an adult man now, well over fifty, but never has he forgotten the pain of that morning when he found CJ and knew his beloved coon had been killed for $35.

Our entire family was really angry for a while but we knew our anger did us no good. It ate up our joy. So we asked God to take care of the problem, to help my brother forget and not hate the man who killed his CJ. Now my brother hopes that someday his own kids will have the joy of a wild coon and he tells them to forgive their enemies, to do good to those who are mean, because hate only hurts yourself.

("I will let no man shrink or belittle my soul by making me hate him.")

Booker T. Washington

Heavenly Father, I praise you for *helping me forgive those who hurt me*

I am thankful today for *The sunshine, that I get to go to Church, new life, I don't have to go to work for 3 weeks*

Please help *Dana, Heath, Ben, Shannon all who are sick with cancer & the Corona Virus, Faye*

Give me this day to walk closer to you, to serve others and to learn all that I need to know to be your child again. In thy Son's name, Amen

March 30 2020

Day Seven

Heavenly Father, I'm here for our appointment., Help me to learn a little bit more today than I knew before. Don't let anything interrupt us. I am trying to love you more. In Jesus's name, Amen.

1 Thessalonians 4:16, 17
For the Lord himself shall descend from heaven with a shout, with the voice of the Archangel and the trumpet of God, and the dead in Christ shall rise first. Then we which are alive and remain shall be caught up together with them in the clouds, to meet the Lord in the air; and so shall we ever be with the Lord.

I really enjoy animals, especially the ones with which I'm able to make friends. One of the animals we've been close to here over the years at Springhaven Croft are our dogs.

Our dogs over the years ranged from tiny to huge and almost nothing in between. Our biggest dog was Admiral Jack of the Kennels of St. John; Hi Jack, for short. He was a champion Newfoundland. He weighed between 170 and 190 pounds depending on how much we'd been able to work him with his wagon. His grandmother was the National Sledge pulling champion: she had pulled 3000 pounds 90 feet in thirty seconds years ago; I've heard the new record is over 10,000 pounds! In winter Hijack tended to put on weight. As a Landseer, he was black and white and friendly. In his younger days we would hitch him to a cart and he would take the kids for rides. He really loved that wagon and when he would see Dan get the harness out he'd run and wait by the cart. He died too early of cancer and we still miss him.

I remember in the spring when he would shed, we'd brush him out and fill several large paper grocery bags of hair. We'd scatter it around the garden for the wild birds and to keep deer out of the garden. The breed was developed in Newfoundland to rescue people who fell off fishing boats and they love to swim. Newfs are the only dog species with true webbed feet. Our problem however, was Jack liked to rescue, too. I remember the time we took him to a farm and he tried to rescue the ducks who just wanted to swim in the pond. Jack had never seen ducks but he knew they had to be saved and we had to tie him up to keep from catching ducks and taking them safely to shore. Once we took him to the Mohican river with us and almost got in trouble as he kept trying to rescue folks who were just lolling around on tires or splashing around enjoying the water. It took a bit to calm all the people down and Jack as well but eventually, they all got to play together with no thought of rescuing.

Newfs are known for having very soft mouths. One time, Dan went out to care for the animals and saw Jack in an interesting behavior. Some sparrows had gotten captured in the dog kennel.. Jack was catching them one by one, going to the door and releasing them. He didn't hurt a one, he just rescued them from a frightening situation, letting them fly free. After they were out, he sat down to wait for his breakfast.. Jack was royalty at heart.

Jack died like all of us someday will and we miss him. Sometimes I get angry about death. If only Adam and Eve had behaved; if only the devil had behaved; if only the Lord would come back right now; but for now we still have sin and sadness and death. Yet the Bible says "I would not have you grieve as they who have no hope." He is coming back soon and He will take us to a place where there is no pain and no death and no sadness. Our part is to wait and be ready and to help others be ready to go as well. Part of that is knowing and accepting God's leading us on our earthly journey: and being willing to be vulnerable and talk to others about Him as well. Another part is to get close enough to God that when it is our time to pass from this old earth, we can look heavenward and have the assurance that He's there waiting for our arrival.

"The second coming of Christ will be so revolutionary that it will change every aspect of life on this planet. Christ will reign in righteousness. Disease will be arrested. Death will be modified. War will be abolished. Nature will be changed. Man will live as it was originally intended he should live."

Billy Graham

Heavenly Father, I praise you for
All the pets I've had & the love they gave me, the money you gave me

I am thankful today for
Parker, Kennedy, Gunner, Denver & Tuff & that I'm healthy & strong enough to keep them

Please help
Scott, Seth, Bradley, Chris

Give me this day to walk closer to you, to serve others and to learn all that I need to know to be your child again. In thy Son's name, Amen

Lord, there's nothing Better than You!

March 31, 2020

Now in this way those who are trusted with something valuable must show they are worthy of that trust.

Day Eight

Heavenly Father, I'm here for our appointment., Help me to learn a little bit more today than I knew before. Don't let anything interrupt us. I am trying to love you more. In Jesus's name, Amen.

I Corinthians 4:2
"Moreover it is required in stewards, that a man be found faithful. "

I find that everything in nature can lead my thoughts to God now; whether they make me laugh at their antics or groan at their messes, they are all lessons to learn more about Him. On our little farm, the other type of breed we've raised has been Pomeranians. We've had several over the years. Poms weigh about 5 to 7 pounds full grown; quite a difference from Jack! While Jack was steady, with a rolling gait, very benevolent over his domain, gentle almost to a fault, Poms bounce and frown and act dignified and are so funny you simply have to laugh at them. Like the time Brother Bear, the sire of our Pom Dynasty, who was ever so dignified (unless asking for a belly rub)got his feelings hurt over some little thing. I believe I scolded him for chewing up the back door mat. He held his little doggie nose high and marched off in high dungeon, did not watch where he was going and promptly fell off the edge of the porch into the bushes. His injured look was more than I could stand and I thought I'd die laughing. He growled at me, extricated himself and trotted off to find his wives to commiserate about the unfairness of life. He would not come up to be petted for the rest the afternoon.

Another pom was called Sunnybear. She was friendly except when she had puppies and then she'd eat your leg off if you came near the nestbox . I remember when the puppies were near the stage at which they learned to walk as being really hilarious. They would growl fiercely to anyone who came into their territory. They would attack ferocious shoelaces and shake them to submission. They'd hide in the closet and go to sleep in your shoes. If they were a bigger dog, they'd be dangerous. Since they were only 6 or 8 inches long they were simply just ridiculous. Another female was Snowybear, white and always into something. She used to eat my crocus bulbs faster than I could plant them. She stomped the flowers over, dug out the bulbs and ate them as fast as they could bloom. I had to put chicken wire over my flower bed. She didn't seem to like tulips, she was indifferent to daffodils, but oh, she was hard on crocuses.

Pets bring such joy to our lives. To make us laugh and give us a way to learn some responsibility, you simply can't find a better teacher than your animals. I sometimes wonder if Jesus had had a dog as a child. If you have pets remember to treat them kindly. God made us the stewards of the earth not to lord it over and pollute it but to be servants and take care of it. Be a good steward of anything and anyone that He is using you to keep for Him. Everything on earth belongs to Him and He simply loans them to us for a short time to bring us joy, to help us learn and to aid us in knowing more about the home to which we all may go someday.

"Animals are more than ever a test of our character, of mankind's capacity for empathy and for decent, honorable conduct and faithful stewardship. We are called to treat them with kindness, not because they have rights or power or some claim to equality, but in a sense because they don't; because they all stand unequal and powerless before us."

Matthew Scully

Heavenly Father, I praise you for
~~always~~ This day, the rain, Disney

I am thankful today for
Grandbabies, everything

Please help
Scott (Me) Ben, Heath, Judy, Gayle, Lanny, Clint, Stacy

Give me this day to walk closer to you, to serve others and to learn all that I need to know to be your child again. In thy Son's name, Amen

April 1st 2020
Stacy having holder
Whoever loves a brother or sister lives in the light & will not cause anyone to stumble in his faith

Day Nine

Heavenly Father, I'm here for our appointment., Help me to learn a little bit more today than I knew before. Don't let anything interrupt us. I am trying to love you more. In Jesus's name, Amen.

1st John 2:10
"He that loveth his brother abided in the light, and there is no occasion of stumbling in him."

In the lake near me lives the strangest little beast. His name is the caddis fly larva and he's the funniest little fellow. He has a soft body and fears others may eat him before he grows up so he makes a house to carry around. He picks up small pebbles and shells and twigs and takes that debris and glues them to himself till he has covered himself in non-penetrative whole body armor. He looks like a walking recycling center. He seems quite proud of his regalia and marches around occasionally gluing more to it until the day he climbs out of the water, splits his back and flies away as a caddis fly. If you look in a quiet creek and see a small pile of debris walking against the flow, it's probably one of these fellows.

Do you know somebody like that? Someone who has built up a barrier between themselves and the world? Perhaps they are afraid of being gobbled up or hurt, too. Maybe somebody has hurt them before and they're afraid to let anyone close to them again. Sometimes they come across not as shy but as curmudgeons. I know a lot of old folks that way. So afraid of meeting the world and being harmed or taken advantage of they act crabby as a grizzly out of season. They hear the news reports of all the violence and scams and bad things happening to seniors they've decided to survive they need to keep everyone at bay. To break their shell isn't simple but if you are patient and kind and friendly to them; try to find a random acts of kindness for them; be consistent in your good mornings and sharing of yourself, you can open them up.

If you practice kindness to others, they may find the shell they have built will feel too tight and they will want to shed it and become a friend to you. Ask God to give you ideas of ways you can help them feel more comfortable.

Or maybe you've built barriers around your own heart because of someone's cruelty. There's a fear inside when you think of meeting new folks or trying new things. Don't give up on everyone because of bullies or hateful folks. Hold your head up, walk tall, you are a child of God, a member of the Royal family, and you can stand tall and smile. There is a lot to be said about appearing confident and eventually feeling that way. My son used to say "Fake it til you make it." As a therapist, I can agree with that to a degree. If you act brave, step out and try, even if just to stand straighter and smile, people will treat you differently. Give life a chance to be good. If you find you are the one with a barrier, ask Him to find a safe way to remove it, to lower it, to grow in His grace and in self-confidence. With His help and your willingness, your shy friend will grow into a happy friend. Your own fear will be less and you will be able to share your faith with others.

The world will be better because you let yourself shine in it, in whatever sphere you live in.

"Friendship can weather most things and thrive in thin soil - but it needs a little mulch of letters and phone calls and small silly presents every so often - just to save it from drying out completely."
Pam Brown

Heavenly Father, I praise you for
new life !! for keeping me out of my shell

I am thankful today for
Grandbabies! Sunshine my soft bed. That you are shutting the door on the Corona Virus

Please help
Stacy, Haley, Dr Hurd, Hustin Tuff Bo Clint, Ben, Heath, Faye, Barbara, Dana

Give me this day to walk closer to you, to serve others and to learn all that I need to know to be your child again. In thy Son's name, Amen

April 2 2000

Day Ten

Heavenly Father, I'm here for our appointment., Help me to learn a little bit more today than I knew before. Don't let anything interrupt us. I am trying to love you more. In Jesus's name, Amen.

Psalms 23:6
Surely goodness and mercy shall follow me all the days of my life and I shall dwell in the house of the Lord forever.

The scientists at the Brigham Young Women's Hospital in Boston have discovered kangaroos. Lest you think they have a leak in the brain bucket, let me clarify that statement. Dr. Stephen Ringer, the director of newborn services, did some experiments with premature infants. In past years they would've been put in an incubator until they were stronger and larger and able to survive. But Dr. Ringer has discovered that by taking the babies out of the incubator and placing them skin to skin, chest to chest, in their mother's arms, they grow faster, fidget less, maintain body temperature and gain weight better. In short, he's making the mothers of premies into temporary marsupials.

It makes total sense if you think it through. The babies have been listening to their mother's voice and her heartbeat in the womb for 6 or 7 or 8 months and hearing her again makes them happier and more secure. They know mama is near and mama will take care of them and they relax. They're much better able to survive and a relaxed baby survives better. The babies bond to mom; they attach to her smell and her heart and her care. The mom attaches to the baby easier and there are less problems with postnatal depression. The system is called kangarooing after the pouch in which marsupials nurture their young.

Premature babies and us have much in common. Here on this old earth we're in a terminal state. Both of us can benefit from being heart-to-heart with our parents; babies to mama and us to God. We need to cuddle close and feel secure in His love. We need help to grow strong. And someday, when the Lord returns, we will recognize His face, His voice, His love. After all, we've heard His heartbeat before; we've felt His voice within. We will grow up in His new world.

The love and caring of the Great Designer and Creator of the universe gives me hope. It gives me a feeling of safety and it provides a rock to attach the chain of my heart to, and know I cannot be shaken by world events or personal crisis. I have One who is always there.

"The most important thing for me is having a relationship with God. To know that the owner, the creator of the universe loves you, sent His Son to die for your sins; that's very empowering. Knowing Him and knowing that He loves me gives me encouragement and confidence to

move forward."
Benjamin Carson

Heavenly Father, I praise you for
Loving me + Sending your son to die for my sins

I am thankful today for
New life, answered prayer, friends, my family

Please help
Scott, my attitude, me to Love You more & Be more like You.

Give me this day to walk closer to you, to serve others and to learn all that I need to know to be your child again. In thy Son's name, Amen

April 3 2020 — The right word spoken at the right time is as beautiful as gold apples in a silver bowl

Day Eleven

Heavenly Father, I'm here for our appointment., Help me to learn a little bit more today than I knew before. Don't let anything interrupt us. I am trying to love you more. In Jesus's name, Amen.

Proverbs 25:11. A word fitly spoken is like apples of gold in pictures of silver.

Once upon a time, we had a horse, or I should say a colt. She was about 2 years old when Dad decided it was high time to start training her. Up until now, her days had been spent running around in the field with her mother, eating grass, kicking up her heels, doing whatever came into her head. It was time she learned proper horse manners.

So Dad called the mother horse into the barn and the colt, named Star, followed her right along. He got the mom into a stall and gave her oats, then captured Star. First Dad slipped a halter over Star's head and fastened it firmly. That didn't bother her too much. Then he attached a lead rope and begin to lead her into a corral; now that bothered her. She planted her feet and begin to pull back on the rope. Dad was ready. My older brother had a willow switch, and he stood just behind her. When she walked with Dad nothing happened except she was given pieces of carrot on a regular basis. When she planted her feet, Mike switched her one time on her rump which surprised her so much she would trot forward. As soon as she moved forward, she would be given a carrot again. It didn't take her too long to discover carrots are better than switches and she walked nicely on lead.

    Dad put a saddle blanket on her and an empty saddle. You would have thought he dropped a wasp nest on her! She reared, she bucked, she squealed! And it didn't do her any good. Dad had fastened her halter to a training post and he was a master at fastening on saddles and she couldn't get rid of it. After a while, she kicked herself tired. Dad came up to her with more carrots, gentle petting and led her around on lead. After a while he took the saddle off. The next day, he put it on again and she didn't fight quite so much. In 3 or 4 days, she didn't fight it at all and dad started tying feed sacks to the saddle to give it a little weight. Step-by-step, he gentled Star. Her fussing and fighting did her no good. She learned to accept a rider and she was a good, obedient horse. We children got a lot of enjoyment from riding that horse, and Dad eventually sold her to an older gentleman who wanted her for his grandchildren.

    Have you been gentled? Have you learned to say please and thank you and excuse me? Have you learned to put the cell phone down when in conversation so you can look folks in the eye and give them the attention needed to hold a good conversation? Have you learned the famous rule, "<u>Good manners in seven words be found, forget yourself and think of those around?</u>" True Christians will be among the gentlest and kindest and politest of people. <u>Jesus was never rude.</u> I'm sure he said thank you and excuse me and pardon me and forgive me. It heaven people will not be stubborn, argumentative, angry, or selfish. If we aren't that way in heaven, shouldn't you be learning good manners now? You will be much more useful to God and everyone will like you better if you learn to think of others first, and treat everyone with kindness. A person able to be gentle to others, while standing firmly on principle is a power in this world. It takes nothing to lose your temper and fuss; it takes strength to be gentle.

"Rudeness is the weak man's imitation of strength."
                                                    Eric Hoffer

Heavenly Father, I praise you for
growing me everyday Sunshine & warmth

I am thankful today for
Grandbabies, family, that you give me everything I need Blessings, Gifts,

Please help
Dann, Scott, Ben, Judy, Gayle, Cammy, Clint, Bo, Faye, Barbara, Me,

Give me this day to walk closer to you, to serve others and to learn all that I need to know to be your child again. In thy Son's name, Amen

I Love you Lord,

April 4th 2020

Day Twelve

Heavenly Father, I'm here for our appointment., Help me to learn a little bit more today than I knew before. Don't let anything interrupt us. I am trying to love you more. In Jesus's name, Amen.

Genesis 1:26 Let us make man in our image, after our likeness: and let him have dominion over the fish of the sea, the fowl of the air, and over the cattle, and over all the earth, and over every creeping thing that creeps upon the earth.

There is a gorgeous little finch aptly named the lady Gouldian Finch. Back in 1844, Sir John Gould , the first European who had seen this bird named the little bird after his wife, lady Gould.

Gouldians have different patches of color on them; it may be green, red, yellow, white, purple and black or any dilution of the same. All of them on the same little bird makes them very easy to spot in the world of aviaries and bird cages as they're incredibly gaudy. In their native habitat, it's a form of camouflage. You see, they live among the flowering grasslands in their native country od Australia. God saw fit to camouflage them with bright colors. They blend right in with the flower plants.

In nature, Gouldians build their nests in hollow trees. In the aviary, Gouldians build a tunnel nest. It's made of piles and piles of dried grass which they burrow into sometimes as far back as 3 feet! Imagine a haystack with several long tunnels built back into it and you'll just about have it pictured correctly. The tunnels are dark, so much so that parents can't see to feed the babies in the dark. So God gave them an interesting way to find the baby mouths to feed them. The babies mouths glow in the dark! I am not kidding. They have 2 dots of glowing green on either side of their beaks in the back. The parent aims the food between the dots and the baby is fed. When the baby is old enough to fledge out, the glowing quits. He can't be found to feed so he comes out looking for food, falls out, and flies away.

Isn't God amazing? He has made so many interesting forms of life. He could have just made robins all over the world to eat the excess worms but instead He patiently thought out thousands of kinds of birds; all of which we could study and learn about. He has given us plenty to do just in studying the animals and birds here on earth to keep us busy for lifetimes of years. When He returns, we'll all have all the time we need to learn about all of nature on this planet and wherever else we chose to study. Our Angels will be there to help us study and learn. The homeschool in heaven is going to be awesome. Why not start studying nature now? You can study all the way to heaven and back.

"Doth not all nature around me praise God? If I were silent, I should be an exception to the universe. Doth not the thunder praise Him as it rolls like drums in the march of the God of armies? Do not the mountains praise Him when the woods upon their summits wave in adoration? Doth not the lightning write His name in letters of fire? Hath not the whole earth a voice? And shall I, can I, silent be?"

Charles Spurgeon

Heavenly Father, I praise you for
nature, & all the animals & Birds

I am thankful today for
a free day! going fishing, Your peace, mercy & Grace

Please help
everyone Lord & heal us & our (land) (World)

Give me this day to walk closer to you, to serve others and to learn all that I need to know to be your child again. In thy Son's name, Amen

*April 5 2020
Palm Sunday*

He has put his angels in charge of you to watch over you wherever you go.

Day Thirteen

Heavenly Father, I'm here for our appointment., Help me to learn a little bit more today than I knew before. Don't let anything interrupt us. I am trying to love you more. In Jesus's name, Amen.

Psalms 91:11
For he shall give his angels charge over thee, to keep thee in all thy ways.

One of my favorite animals is baby goats. We used to have pygmy goats when my children were small. At first I wanted goats just to clean up the field so we could have a horse. You see, I had read that goats eat multiflora roses and other plants that are bad for horses, so I decided a couple goats would be useful. Being an organic farmer, I don't like to use chemicals and I avoid them whenever I can.

I looked at adults, but they didn't seem to be very tame, so I decided if we raised them from kids, they would be easier to handle and safer for my children. I put an ad in a local paper and a lady called me saying she had day old kids. We went to see them and we all fell in love. Baby pygmy goats are a foot tall and weigh under a pound. They have long eyelashes and they like to be held. If you hold them in your arms, they naturally snuggle up under your chin. They are soft and friendly and ever so cute. We quickly found them endearing.

We bought two and we took them home where for the next 3 weeks we hand fed them. At first it was a really bad job and I wondered if I'd done the right thing in bringing them home so young. The lady I bought them from at the farm had told me that the parents had refused to take care of them since they were each one of triplets, so we just stuck it out. We had to feed them every 3 hours all day and all night long. I even took them in a basket to my college classes! They slept quietly in the basket and between classes, I fed them their bottle and let them run around in the lawn. They'd soon tire and I'd snuggle them back to their basket bed and put them to sleep. We gradually lengthened the time between feedings to 4 hours and then started giving them grass and grain. When they were 3 weeks old we took them outside to play for the first time in the barnyard.

First thing out of their basket they thought our Newfoundland dog Jack was a mother goat. They tried to find his milk spigots. He got disgusted and lay down. Then they decided he was a mountain and took turns running up his back and jumping off his head. We had to put a stop to that because even though Jack was a patient dog, he did have his limits. We took them for a walk in the field that would eventually be their home. Baby goats bounce straight up in the air like they have springs for knees. Straight up and then bouncing just like Tigger in Winnie the Pooh is called spronging. It's a delight to watch. But as my own children grew up, we grew out of needing the horse or the goats so we no longer have them. In the spring sometimes, I can still see in my mind's eye those little goats spronging across the field, their mother patiently eating poison ivy and multiflora roses and thistles and all the noxious weeds that they loved so much. I really like goats.

I suspect our guardian angels are a little like that. I believe when somebody is born God assigns him an angel. That Angel is there watching and protecting as they learn to walk; smiling proudly the first time these say Jesus, worrying over them on their first date, smiling when they're happy, comforting them when they're sad. When someone's person passes away, God tells the Angel to mark where he is buried. At that great resurrection day, when the Angels are sent to bring us all home your Angel will hurry to where you were buried to greet us as we rise. You will finally see the one who's been caring for you all these years.

An you image the scene when all those angels escort their persons to meet Jesus, and then shows them around heaven, so happy and so proud that he's finally home and safe. Can you imagine the sadness of the angel whose person doesn't go to heaven? When the other Angels are happily showing their friends all the joys of the heavenly city, he has to live with the fact that his person didn't value his own life enough to care about heaven. Throughout eternity your Angel will miss you so dearly if you decide not to go. When you decide to let nothing come between you and God so that someday you will have the joy of meeting your Angel and he will have the joy of showing you your mansion and the tree of life and the golden streets and the planets and the stars and best of all, our friend, Jesus, heaven must break into singing.

"We may speak about a place where there are no tears, no death, no fear, no night; but those are just the benefits of heaven. The beauty of heaven is seeing God."
Max Lucado

Heavenly Father, I praise you for
My Angel, Your son Jesus, music. I praise you that I (get) to go to church today.

I am thankful today for
New life, the birds singing outside my window, for your peace.

Please help
all 1st responders, Bradley, Health care workers, all who are sick & needy.

Give me this day to walk closer to you, to serve others and to learn all that I need to know to be your child again. In thy Son's name, Amen

April 6, 2020
Holy week

Day Fourteen

Heavenly Father, I'm here for our appointment., Help me to learn a little bit more today than I knew before. Don't let anything interrupt us. I am trying to love you more. In Jesus's name, Amen.

2 Peter 3:18
But grow in grace, and in the knowledge of our Lord and Savior, Jesus Christ.

A young girl in a revival meeting was filled with love for her Lord and the desire to help someone be saved. She looked around and saw a distinguished looking gentleman with a frown on his face. She bustled up to him and said, "Sir, are you saved?"

He stiffened and said sternly, "Young lady, I am a bishop!"

The girl was unfamiliar with the term, so she smiled and said, "That's all right, sir, God can even save bishops!"

Isn't wonderful that anyone can receive the gift of life? Jesus Christ, our righteousness, calls everyone to Him, no matter what their station in life. He is always there, waiting for us to want him. He is our total answer to the problem of sin. He forgives our sins, and He enables us to forgive ourselves and to succeed where we have failed before. I hope that in reading this devotional, you are learning more about His grace, His righteousness and to learn how to find lessons in everything He has created..

I love to collect stories. One of my favorite stories is about a group of European children during World War II. They made uniforms as best they could in those bad times, and they learned to march and drill. They hated Hitler and what he had done to their country. One day they staged a little parade through town, right after their area had been shelled again by the Germans. Holding a banner high that said, "Youth for a Free Europe," they walked through the demoralized town, shouting, "Look out, Hitler! We are growing up!" Their brave protest gave hope back to that little town.

In my mind's eye, I can see an army of youth learning to trust God in growing in grace. I see all of them praying and growing and learning to do whatever it takes to reach the world, and I see all of us as children in God's eyes, learning and growing, trusting in His goodness and in His love, and sharing that love with our neighbors and family. I hear a huge swelling of hearts crying out: "Look out, devil! Our kids are growing up! And you are a beaten enemy!"

The journey we are on is not long. The trip has bumps and starts, fits and frustration, but all of us, no matter how old or young, are learning to trust.

> "The greatest want of the world is the want of men – men who will not be bought or sold; men who

in their inmost souls are true and honest; men who do not fear to call sin by its right name; men whose conscience is as true to duty as the needle to the pole; men who will stand for the right though the heavens fall."

Ellen G. White

Heavenly Father, I praise you for _showing me in your Grace, the storm this world is going through today. Time off_

I am thankful today for _Time off, your son, the storms of life, friends & family, new life_

Please help _all who are lonely & scared, sick, worried & fearful, Scott, Beverly, Randy, Barbara, Faye, Tom, Deborah, John, Rachel, Dr Thomas, Nelly_

Give me this day to walk closer to you, to serve others and to learn all that I need to know to be your child again. In thy Son's name, Amen

Lord theres nothing Better Than You

April 7 2020
Where God's love is, there is no fear because God's perfect love drives out fear. It is punishment that makes a person fear, so love is not made perfect in the person who fears

Day Fifteen

Heavenly Father, I'm here for our appointment., Help me to learn a little bit more today than I knew before. Don't let anything interrupt us. I am trying to love you more. In Jesus's name, Amen.

1 John 4:18 there is no fear in love but perfect love casts out fear, because fear hath torment. He did fear it is not made perfect in love.

I had a science teacher once whose name was Mr. Ache(pronounced aw- key). He was a returning missionary on furlough. He had caught malaria so badly that he had to come home for a while so he was teaching in my public school. He had so many great stories to tell! One that impressed me was one about the soldiers.

He had been asked to work in unentered territory in Africa. He wanted to take the gospel to a certain tribe that had never been reached before. With Bible and food in his knapsack, his wife right behind, and some native couriers carrying bundles and showing the way to the village, he started out. About half way to the village, his native helpers put down all the bundles and said they could go no farther because this was the end of their territory and they weren't going farther. He would have to go it alone. They said that the tribes in this area of the jungle were very uncivilized and had the bad habit of eating those people they didn't like and they weren't interested in being dinner!

Mr. Ache tried to reason with them but to no avail. They left. So he and his wife rearranged the bundles that they might be able to handle, bundled the others up a tree, and started out again for the hike into the woods. Mr. Ache said he felt like someone was watching him but he saw nobody. He and his wife prayed several times and moved on.

The oddest thing happened. When he and his wife finally arrived in the village, they were greeted as friends. They were given a place to stay; all their other packages were brought to them and already in the hut! He couldn't have been more surprised. Mr. Ache spoke several dialects and he tried several before he found somebody who could translate their conversation and they paid him to be an interpreter. Mr. Ache told them the story of the gospel. They listened remarkably well and asked to hear more. He and his wife stayed for several weeks.

One day the chief asked him if the soldiers would be coming back to take them home soon. Mr. Ache was baffled since the mission compound had no soldiers and no one had come with them. But the chief insisted that when Mr. Ache and his wife had first come to the village they were surrounded by a band of bright shining soldiers all around. The soldiers were smiling so they knew they were friendly, and they also knew they shouldn't mess with Mr. Ache. The lead soldier had gone on ahead of them and told them they must show the missionaries every kindness and listen to what they said because the Great One in the sky said they must do so. As soon as he had given this message, all the soldiers vanished just as Mr. Ache and his wife came in the village. The soldiers came back every night and circled the hut where Mr. Ache and his wife stayed. Now that the missionary was going to leave would they see the shining ones again, the chief inquired? Mr. Ache told them that if the Great God of heaven wanted them to see the shining soldiers they'd see them. He and his wife left the village. When he left, the villagers were building a church. He doesn't know whether they saw shining soldiers again or not. But today there's a small jungle church among a tribe that were once cannibals because God loved them enough to send angels to help them learn.

"Safety comes in our nearness to God, not in our distance from our enemies."

Dillon Burroughs

Heavenly Father, I praise you for
Sending Change your angels to watch over me and my family

I am thankful today for
Another Day That I am yours My Knee is Better

Please help
me & my attitude, Scott, Heath, Ben, Judy, Gayle, Lanny, Clint, Bo, Seth, Elliott & Ponda

Give me this day to walk closer to you, to serve others and to learn all that I need to know to be your child again. In thy Son's name, Amen

April 8th 2020
John + Rachel Baby

And I tell you that on the judgment day people will be responsible for every careless thing they have said

Day Sixteen

Heavenly Father, I'm here for our appointment., Help me to learn a little bit more today than I knew before. Don't let anything interrupt us. I am trying to love you more. In Jesus's name, Amen.

Matthew 12:36
But I say to you that for every idle word men may speak, they will give account of it in the day of judgment.

You can never be too careful about public address systems, as one sound engineer learned the hard way.

He was hired to wire up a hall for a series of revival meetings. He had to be there the first night to be sure everything went well. He thought he had it right, but he had to wait until the pastor began to speak to do the last mic check. He really wanted to be home and not have to listen to the sermon. Sermons made him nervous. He wasn't a saved person; he simply hadn't thought about it. He was there to do a job, that was it.

There was a crowd of four thousand people in the hall. The pastor in charge was an older gentleman. He was a little anxious, and he was slow in getting his sermon going. He fiddled with the mic, he shuffled his notes, he turned to his first verse, he took a drink of water. The engineer was irked by the delay, and he spoke out loud in the sound booth, "Hurry up, you old goat!"

The engineer didn't realize he had the sound room mic on, but all four thousand people and the speaker knew all about it. The tension in the meeting was broken up with laughter, the pastor got over his nervousness, and the meeting was a success, but the engineer never really lived it down among the community. Years later, he is a practicing Christian and he laughs about it now but at the time….

Something we as Christians should realize is that the mic is always on between us and God. Every word we speak is heard by heaven. You use profanity, but think that your family doesn't know, so it's okay? Think again! The universe has a parabolic mic turned in on you, and you're going to hear the recording played back some day in the judgment! Don't say anything you will be ashamed of hearing again in front of the universe. One of my friends used to say not to say anything that you will regret later. Keep your language sweet and if you have to take it back it won't taste as bad.

> "Progress means getting nearer to the place you want to be. And if you have taken a wrong turning, then to go forward does not get you any nearer.
> "If you are on the wrong road, progress means doing an about-turn and walking back to the right road; and in that case the man who turns back soonest is the most progressive man."
> –C.S. Lewis

Heavenly Father, I praise you for
Loving me + never giving up on me

I am thankful today for
your peace, the calm, being off work, family & friends

Please help
Scott, Dany, my attitude, my mouth, John + Rachel, baby seal, all who are sick

Give me this day to walk closer to you, to serve others and to learn all that I need to know to be your child again. In thy Son's name, Amen

April 9 2020
Maunday Thursday
Give all your worries to him because He cares about you

Page Seventeen

Heavenly Father, I'm here for our appointment., Help me to learn a little bit more today than I knew before. Don't let anything interrupt us. I am trying to love you more. In Jesus's name, Amen.

1 Peter 5:7
Casting all your care upon Him, for He cares for you.

Worry, worry, worry, stress, stress and more stress – that's what daily life can sometimes feel like.

No matter what our best intentions are, we never seem to find time to relax and unwind our troubled minds. We want to spend time with our families, but we have to pay the rent, the utilities, the car insurance, Bobby needs shoes and Sally needs a costume for school, and we need to cut coupons and we need to, and need to, and need to . . . meanwhile, our lives are dashing away from us, and we hardly know what enjoying life means anymore. We keep trading our precious time here on earth for what?

A country song I heard recently had as its' chorus,

> I'm in a hurry to get things done
> and I rush and rush until life's no fun
> all I really need to do is live and die
> but I'm in a hurry and don't know why

(Alabama, 1992)

Is your life like that?

Jesus told us to consider the lilies and how they grow, and the sparrows that fly everywhere. He asked the crowd who takes care of them, yet they survive and they even thrived on what seemed to be a lack of care from anyone. He told us to consider the beauty of the lilies of the field(I like to imagine them as daylilies like we have here in Ohio.) They don't work, they just sit there in the field, blooming, swaying in the breeze, making the world a lovely place. He told us to attend to nature because it can teach us so much; like how not to worry.

Have you ever looked at simplifying your life? Is everything on your to-do (or to-acquire) list really so direly needed that it is worth trading your life for it?
Consider asking yourself, "Is this thing I want worth this many hours of my life to get?" Money is actually just an intermediary used for trading hours of your life for an object or a need. Is the thing you are considering worth a piece of your life to obtain?

And if it is worth the money, in the grand story of the redemption of this planet, will it really matter whether you drove a Chevy or a Beamer in the end? Will the thing stand between you and God, or is it likely to cause someone else to covet and start running madly around trying to match it?

Think about simplifying your life to what's really important. Is it the TV ball game, or a child's request to read to them more important to you? Watching the

Olympics or helping at a shelter? Ask God His opinion. Find what is really important, and live simpler.

You won't regret stepping out of the endless hamster wheel of modern life and resting for a short time.

"He who created us without our help will not save us without our consent."
St. Augustine

Heavenly Father, I praise you for
Sending your son Jesus to die for me

I am thankful today for
time by myself, That you are shutting down the Corona Virus That You are in Control

Please help
me, Scott, Rachel, Pat Teresa Tanya & Kevin all who are sick

Give me this day to walk closer to you, to serve others and to learn all that I need to know to be your child again. In thy Son's name, Amen

April 10 2020
Good Friday

Do not think you are better than you are. You must decide what you really are by the amount of faith God has given you.

Day Eighteen

Heavenly Father, I'm here for our appointment., Help me to learn a little bit more today than I knew before. Don't let anything interrupt us. I am trying to love you more. In Jesus's name, Amen.

Romans 12:3
For I say, through the grace given to me, to everyone who is among you, not to think of himself more highly than he ought to think, but to think soberly, as God has dealt to each one a measure of faith.

You have seen them before, those beautiful people who simply think they are the hottest item on the menu? We shake our heads and roll our eyes at the self-centered attitude and lifestyle. It reminds me of an old Native story, and since I am a native storyteller, I thought it might teach us all something.

Kunakwat, lowat, nuchink, many moons ago, as my grandfather told to me, when the four-leggeds and winged brothers controlled Turtle Island, there was a tribe of creatures who wanted to have a powwow.

"I shall gather wood for the fire," said the beaver. Everyone nodded their heads and agreed it was good.

"I shall be the drum," said a prairie chicken rooster, beating on his chest. Again, all agreed that it was good.

"I will be the lead dancer," declared the rooster. And everyone rolled their eyes but agreed, to keep the peace of the tribe.

You see, this old rooster was so proud of his looks and especially of his tail, shining and blue-black in the sun, draping gracefully behind him it had gotten annoying to just about everyone. His hens followed him around and flirted with him, and he felt sure everyone knew that he was the most lovely bird in the land. He was certain no one had ever seen anyone strut like himself, no one could dance so fine as he. Pretty much everyone was tired of his pride, but they were too polite to say so, and felt it easier to just let him have his way; they'd still have a good powwow if they went into it with a good spirit in their hearts.

So the day of the powwow began, and the fire in the ring was burning and sending up sparks. Everyone lined up for the Grand Entry, with the rooster and his shy little hens leading the way. In he marched, strutted and stepping high, bowing to the drummers, and prancing around. He noticed that when he got closer to the fire, his tail and neck feathers sparkled like ripples on water on a sunny day, so he swirled around, sweeping his tail. The other animals started to gasp and shake their heads and he thought they were praising his ever-so-fine looks.

But what they were trying to tell him was that his tail was on fire! He finally smelt something bad, looked around, and saw the flames. Have you ever smelled burning feathers? It's decidedly smelly. To try and put them out, he jumped up and started to fly, which just fanned his tail fire, and it got brighter and brighter, higher and higher until he was just a shooting star across the sky.

Now, listen, if you are as proud as that rooster, someday, something will happen to bring you down – it might be fire, it might be illness, it might be something else. The Lord does not like us to be prideful. Remember the rooster, and remember it is better to be humble than proud.

> "A world of nice people, content in their own niceness, looking no further, turned away from God, would be just as desperately in need of salvation as a miserable world – and might be even more difficult to save."
>
> C.S. Lewis

Heavenly Father, I praise you for

Changing me little by little every day I'm not there yet but one day I will!

I am thankful today for

new life in Baby seal "Sunshine" The restoring of my family

Please help

The Seal Family please restore them Haley, my attitude

Give me this day to walk closer to you, to serve others and to learn all that I need to know to be your child again. In thy Son's name, Amen

April 11 2020 — Love each other like brothers & sisters. Give each other more honor than you want for yourselfs

Day Nineteen

Heavenly Father, I'm here for our appointment., Help me to learn a little bit more today than I knew before. Don't let anything interrupt us. I am trying to love you more. In Jesus's name, Amen.

Romans 12:10
Love one another with brotherly affection. Outdo one another in showing honor.

Have you ever spent time in a well-run preschool? By and large, the kids get along; they might squabble now and then over a toy, but they forget the squabble quickly when redirected, and they play together, hold hands on their way to the playground, and in general direct their energy to exercise, not harming one another.

Somewhere along second or third grade, kids start learning to discriminate; suddenly the little kid with dark skin or slanted eyes, who dresses in old clothes or who has a facial tic starts getting picked on. In a good school, ostracizing the different kid is addressed properly; but on the playground, and on the walk home after school, the bullying goes on.

Fly forward a few years. High school, the cliques have formed. Nerds go here, Hispanic goes here, preps go here, hulks go here. The lone child who fits none of the above, be they an Aspie kid, an LD kid, a poor kid; they have no place to go. They learn to be inconspicuous so no one notices them enough to say one more bad thing. The different kids ego takes a beating.

After graduation, the lonely, different ones will either fade away into the world of drugs or low paying jobs or suicide. Research has shown that those who had just one supportive person in their lives go to college or into a trade; they start their own business; they own a resilience to hold on and fight. They still have a lonely, empty spot in their soul where friends were supposed to have been, but they're successful in the world's eyes. High school reunion time, you hear things like "Wow! Look at Joe! Never thought he'd manage all that." And they still don't talk to him.

It hurts worse to see this pattern in homeschoolers and Christian schools and dare I say churches? We ought to know better. We ought to be teaching our kids that heaven is an all-inclusive place; it only requires Christ in our hearts to enter. I've lived long enough now, and studied professionally now, and observed that even in our churches and our homes, the faith of Christ has not made the changes needed in our souls to help us be accepting of all people. How it must make God weep!

Today as you go about your normal life, think of those around you and make an effort to look for the one who is lonely, who sits apart; search them out and be kind to them. Should a follower of Christ do less?

"I like your Christ, I do not like your Christians. Your Christians are so unlike your Christ."
                                    Mahatma Gandhi

Heavenly Father, I praise you for
Sunshine, music, another day, everything

I am thankful today for
new life, another day, you, Love, Grace & Mercy

Please help
me change to be more like you, all who don't know you, all who are lonely, sick, hurt, needy, hungry

Give me this day to walk closer to you, to serve others and to learn all that I need to know to be your child again. In thy Son's name, Amen

April 12 2020
EASTER!!!

Day Twenty

Heavenly Father, I'm here for our appointment., Help me to learn a little bit more today than I knew before. Don't let anything interrupt us. I am trying to love you more. In Jesus's name, Amen.

1 Corinthians 10:13
No temptation has overtaken you that is not common to man. God is faithful, and he will not let you be tempted beyond your ability, but with the temptation he will also provide the way of escape, that you may be able to endure it.

I remember the story of an old deacon who always seem to pray the same prayer. He always ended this prayer with, "and Lord, clean the cobwebs out of my life." It got to be such a habit, it really irritated people. Of course, the old man meant he wanted the Lord to get rid of the things that really shouldn't be there in the first place since they gathered in his heart during the week. Still, people got imitated by it, so much so that one Sabbath, after his favorite take out the cobwebs speech, an elder spoke up and said, "Forget the cobwebs already! Kill the spider!"

Isn't that what needs to be done in our lives? We seem often to have one habitual sin that we keep asking forgiveness for, week after week, and never seem to be able to resist. Perhaps we been asking for God to clear the cobwebs when what we need to do is ask him to kill the desire spider that spins webs, weakening you until your fail into error again and to give into the temptation. That spider of selfishness in our lives needs to go. Do you have an insect problem in your soul? God is a great exterminator!

("If a man cannot be a Christian in the place he is, he cannot be a Christian anywhere.")

Henry Ward Beecher

Heavenly Father, I praise you for *This Day, Your Son Jesus + what He did for all of us to give us life!*

I am thankful today for *Getting to going to Church (everything)*

Please help *Eric, Scott, My Attitude (Judgemental)*

Give me this day to walk closer to you, to serve others and to learn all that I need to know to be your child again. In thy Son's name, Amen

April 13 2020

Day Twenty-one

Heavenly Father, I'm here for our appointment., Help me to learn a little bit more today than I knew before. Don't let anything interrupt us. I am trying to love you more. In Jesus's name, Amen.

Exodus 14:13 -14
And Moses said to the people, "Fear not, stand firm, and see the salvation of the Lord, which he will work for you today. For the Egyptians whom you see today, you shall never see again.

Recently, I thought I had my day planned out. Get up, care for the pets, pack a lo carb lunch, head out for the office, put in my day, come home, start the laundry, take a good cardio walk, make supper, ease into my normal writing routine. Up there is heaven, God had other plans. Today was going to be a test of the "Jeanette-Are-You-Listening-to-Heaven-Network." And there is no loud siren letting you know it's happening, no real announcement that for the next few minutes, there was a test going on for use in emergencies, just to be sure the machinery acted like it ought to.

The canaries were fine, crabby in their winter molt, but healthy. However, the dogs refused to use their potty run for what it was supposed to be used for and when let back inside, promptly managed to both have diarrhea on the newly shampooed rug (last night's after work project!). I made rice for them, mixed it with some chicken and put them in their cages. I cleaned the rug, set it to soak with spot cleaner.

I went to pack my lo carb lunch to find out we didn't have pickles to eat with the cheese. So I substituted olives. (I am not really fond of them but hey, lo carb.) I grabbed a bowl of granola and headed out. I got into the car to drive to the office and it wouldn't start; husband had to jump it.

I got to the office and found the furnace was out so I had to run home for a heater to keep the therapy room warm; with a note from my suite mate found on my desk saying the furnace had died last Friday and they guy was coming tomorrow afternoon to fix it. Three clients canceled at the last minute. Two people in crisis came in. Two different insurance companies refused payment on claims, necessitating a long talk with the billing agency to find out what happened.

I rushed home after seeing all the clients and the dogs were better so took them on a walk; neither liked the snow and after I got to the back fence refused to walk in the snow and I had to carry them home (Pomeranians can be wimps!). The dryer was making a weird noise and wouldn't heat up properly. One of our barn cats had kittens in the hay barn in the middle of winter. This is not kitten weather!

I went to make supper and found out I was out of potatoes. By now, I was feeling out of sorts as well. I went to switch loads in the washer and nearly tripped over one of our basement cats. (I have a tendency to bring my smaller outside animals indoors in winter.)

I changed out the laundry and as I trudged up the basement steps, I was really fussing at God. I heard nothing until I turned the corner into the living room and a sudden thought occurred to me; I had not only been grumpy, I'd forgotten to pray. All day I'd been trying to do this on my own. I'd even forgotten my usual worship. I mean, if you don't ask Him to help, you tie His hands.

I have never felt quite so foolish-all these little problems could have been blessings, but I'd allowed them to stir me up way beyond what they were worth. I went to my study corner, bent my head and apologized. Just at that moment, in late afternoon, all my molting canaries quit scrabbling and began to sing to me. I have them in an aviary, all 22 of them, and they normally sing in the morning, but not during the molt periods. During molt, there is no music. They itch and pull old feathers and crab at each other. This late afternoon, in spite of being in molt, they sang vespers for me, nonstop for thirty minutes as I apologized to my Best Friend for allowing life down here make me miss my appointment with Life up there. And when they quit singing, I got up and made supper, which turned out just fine without the potatoes. He just had to get my attention and I learned sometimes it's the dingy things that wake you up and remind you where your help lies. Outside of Christ, I am weak; in Christ, I am strong.

"Give me this day to walk closer to you, to serve others and to learn all that I need to know to be your child again. In thy Son's name, Amen"

         Watchmen Nee

Heavenly Father, I praise you for
<u>New life! The beautiful Green outside</u>
<u>another day</u>

I am thankful today for
<u>This time with you, another day, everything</u> <u>else</u>
<u>you supply</u>

Please help
<u>Tom, my family, Pat & Teresa's family</u>

Give me this day to walk closer to you, to serve others and to learn all that I need to know to be your child again. In thy Son's name, Amen

April 14, 2020

Then you will have a new name which the Lord himself will give you.

Day Twenty-Two

Heavenly Father, I'm here for our appointment., Help me to learn a little bit more today than I knew before. Don't let anything interrupt us. I am trying to love you more. In Jesus's name, Amen.

Isaiah 62:2
Thou shalt be called a new name, which the mouth of the Lord shall name.

Names, names, names! I can't remember names! Do you have that problem? You are in a new school or church or group. Someone nicely takes you around and introduces everyone to you. In 3 minutes flat, you know nobody's name. Was that blonde kid Jeff or Mac ? Is the pretty brunette Angela or Sue? Don't talk to me, I can't remember your name! And it's so embarrassing! Has that ever happened to you?

Here are some tips I've learned about names. When you are introduced to someone new, keep your mind focused. I ask them to repeat their name if I didn't quite catch it and even if I do since it helps to remember if it's repeated. Most people are flattered you are asking them to repeat it.

Trying to memorize by rote is hard. Dramatize the faces of the names of those you meet. Really, it makes it much simpler to remember that person's name if you can associate another thing to it in your head. Make an exaggeration in your mind -- focus on the face. Think, let's see, the red haired girl with a freckle on her nose is Martí. Her hair is on fire/Marti. The sad, blue eyes of this guy remind me of bluebirds. William bluebird. Don't say it out loud, but it's a fact that the more outrageous the exaggeration, the more likely I am to remember the person. I used to remember my pastor's son's name because he was into saltwater aquariums. I would picture him sitting on a killer whale at Sea world, waving a flag with his name on it. I've never forgotten his name was Bill. I forgot his dad's name and his mom's but the kid is immortalized in my memory.

And another thing; as soon as you can, say the name out loud. As soon as you are introduced, say, "I'm glad I've had a chance to meet you, Bill." Emphasize the name. It's work, but it's a compliment to remember people's name. They are important, and remembering lets them see you feel they are worth knowing.

Aren't you glad we have a God who doesn't have any trouble remembering our names? A God who even knows how many hairs we have on our head? A God who knows our favorite food, sport, pet, school subject -- a God who knows all about us? And who never forgets? Whenever I forget, I am consoled with the thought that someday, I'll have a perfect memory, and a new name. Until then, I'll have to make do with associations and taking special care and being thankful for our God who remembers.

"Someone said that God gave us memories so that we might have roses in December."

J M Barrie

Heavenly Father, I praise you for

my new name, another Day the sunshine simple things

I am thankful today for

this day shoes on my feet, food on my table family & roof over my head

Please help

Tom, Barbara, James Fay, Clint & May Ann Ayla & Ginny Ben & Judy Marty & Donna

Give me this day to walk closer to you, to serve others and to learn all that I need to know to be your child again. In thy Son's name, Amen

April 15 2020 — I am proud of the Good News. Because it is the power God uses to save everyone who believes to save the Jews 1st, it also to save those who are not Jews

Day Twenty-three

Heavenly Father, I'm here for our appointment., Help me to learn a little bit more today than I knew before. Don't let anything interrupt us. I am trying to love you more. In Jesus's name, Amen.

Romans 1:16
I am not ashamed of the gospel of Christ, for it is the power of God to everyone that believe this, to the Jew first and also to the Greek.

The story is told of a French trader in the New Hebrides. He tried to sell the natives whiskey, but they wouldn't buy it. You see, the chieftain was a Christian. So the trader went to argue with the chief. After all, this heathen was cutting into the profit line.

"Bah!," said the trader. "Why are you reading that Bible? I suppose the missionaries gave it to you, you poor fool! Throw away the Bible; it never did anyone any good."

The chief looked up at the trader calmly. He closed his book and said "No? If it weren't for this Bible, you would be cooking in that pot over there for my supper." The trader left in a hurry.

The Bible is our best source for information about God. It tells about his son and his spirit and his wonderful redemption. We'd all be lost without it. Christ our righteousness gave us a precious gift, this Word. Read it every day. It has the power to change you, to bring you so close to God that he will become tangible to you. He wants our love and he tells us so in His Word. Did you know that Christ prayed for you personally, just before his death? Read the prayer of Christ, the last one before He died, memorialized in John 17: here is part of it for you to consider:

John 17:9-26
"I pray for them. I do not pray for the world but for those whom You have given Me, for they are Yours. And all Mine are Yours, and Yours are Mine, and I am glorified in them. Now I am no longer in the world, but these are in the world, and I come to You. Holy Father, keep through Your name those whom You have given Me, that they may be one as We *are.* While I was with them in the world, I kept them in Your name. Those whom You gave Me I have kept; and none of them is lost except the son of perdition, that the Scripture might be fulfilled. But now I come to You, and these things I speak in the world, that they may have My joy fulfilled in themselves. I have given them Your word; and the world has hated them because they are not of the world, just as I am not of the world. I do not pray that You should take them out of the world, but that You should keep them from the evil one. They are not of the world, just as I am not of the world. Sanctify them by Your truth. Your word is truth. As You sent Me into the world, I also have sent them into the world. And for their sakes I sanctify Myself, that they also may be sanctified by the truth. I do not pray for these alone,

but also for those who [i]will believe in Me through their word; **21** that they all may be one, as You, Father, are in Me, and I in You; that they also may be one in Us, that the world may believe that You sent Me. And the glory which You gave Me I have given them, that they may be one just as We are one: I in them, and You in Me; that they may be made perfect in one, and that the world may know that You have sent Me, and have loved them as You have loved Me. Father, I desire that they also whom You gave Me may be with Me where I am, that they may behold My glory which You have given Me; for You loved Me before the foundation of the world. O righteous Father! The world has not known You, but I have known You; and these have known that You sent Me. And I have declared to them Your name, and will declare *it,* that the love with which You loved Me may be in them, and I in them."

He was going to die this week, and his mind was on you. I say again <u>He was getting ready to die, and He thought only of us!</u> He prayed for you. And He left us His Words so we would not wander like a lost child in grocery store, confused and bereft. What an amazing love!

"The Christian life is a life of paradox's. We must give to receive, realize we are blind to see, become simple to be wise, suffer for gain, and die to live."

Unknown

Heavenly Father, I praise you for
This day, Sunshine, new life loving me protecting me from the evil one praying for me Love, grace, mercy

I am thankful today for _your love, Grace & Mercy, your word, you give me everything I need, Family & Friends, Time alone with you_

Please help _my Family draw closer to you_

Give me this day to walk closer to you, to serve others and to learn all that I need to know to be your child again. In thy Son's name, Amen

April 16th 2020 — But respect Christ as the holy Lord in your hearts. Always be ready to answer everyone who ask you to explain about the hope you have.

Day Twenty-four

Heavenly Father, I'm here for our appointment., Help me to learn a little bit more today than I knew before. Don't let anything interrupt us. I am trying to love you more. In Jesus's name, Amen.

1 Peter 3:15
But sanctify the Lord God in your hearts, and always be ready to give a defense to everyone who asks you a reason for the hope that is in you, with meekness and fear;

Are you a person of the Book?

In my childhood, I knew people at our church who were proud to be able to tell you what they believed, and they could back it up with Scripture. I knew an older man, now deceased, who could quote from memory entire books of the Bible (and not just the short ones like Jude; one week, he was called upon to speak in church on short notice. He went up front and said he couldn't think of anything greater than what had already been given us, and then quoted from memory the entire Books of first and second Thessalonians, with small comments here and there. I followed along in my Bible; he missed nary a word.).

However, nowadays, it is a rare person indeed who can give a reason and a rationale for their beliefs other than, that's the way it's always been, or that's what my dad said, or that's what the preacher preached about a couple weeks ago. Or they look at you and try to tell you what the Bible says, and they quote some old proverb that is not scripture at all, or a misquote that changes the meaning of the verse. Let me give you a couple examples.

I had a man swear to me the Bible said "Cleanliness is next to godliness." I can't find it anywhere, not even with a concordance. (With some research, I found it was in a sermon by John Wesley. Last I looked, there is no book of Wesley in Scripture.)

Or what about, "God helps those who help themselves?" Really now, after all the verses in which He says just the opposite about grace being a free gift? (That one dates back to Aesop, though the phrasing is Algernon Sydney, later quoted by Ben Franklin.)

Or how about "Money is the root of all evil"? That's one's a misquote – it's the *love* of money that can cause evil. Or, as the entire passage (1 Timothy 6:6-10) explains, greed leads people to do foolish or harmful things. That is something we've all seen happen.

Ever hear "God helps those who helps themselves?' That's from Aesop's fables, not the Bible.

"To thine own self be true?" That's from Hamlet, in other words, Shakespeare

"A fool and his money are soon parted "is not in Proverbs; it's from Thomas Tusser who wrote it in 1573 in Five Hundreth Pointes of Good Husbandrie.

All these fallacious quotes manage to do is to muddy the waters about salvation and its true source. While it's true that as humans we have doubts sometimes, quoting nonexistent Bible verses is no way to clear those doubts, nor is it a way prove a point.

We need to all become actual readers of His Word, memorizers of His word and we all need to be able to give a reason for what we believe.

"A faith without some doubts is like a human body without antibodies in it. People who blithely go through life too busy or indifferent to ask hard questions about why they believe as they do will find themselves defenseless against either the experience of tragedy or the probing questions of a smart skeptic. "

Tim Keller

Heavenly Father, I praise you for
This day, new life, color

I am thankful today for
your word, friends + family, everything

Please help
Bob Kris, The next Pastor + his family

Give me this day to walk closer to you, to serve others and to learn all that I need to know to be your child again. In thy Son's name, Amen

Congratulations!

If you have faithfully completed the book this far, you have achieved 24 days of transforming your daily visit with God into a lifelong, faith building habit. That is just enough time to have partially extinguished the habit of not having private time with God and to start replacing it with a daily time of caring: you to Him, and He to you. You are well on the way to a closer relationship, a habit of seeking God daily. By getting into the beginnings of a habit to meet with God each day at the same time, in the same place, whether studying the lessons of nature with His help or the thoughts of God through the eyes of others, while seeing a little of His word each day, you are a third of the way to a lifelong friendship.

Let me encourage you at this point to continue: the next section is written to build that friendship and faith with knowledge of His Great Love for you personally. We will still have some nature study, but we go a little more in depth in the next section. In addition, we will dispense with the beginning and ending prayer form since by now you know that and will have been adjusting it to make it your own. Continue this journey knowing His love, His acceptance, His strength and His Spirit will always be there for you. Turn the page, and let's walk in His light.

Handwritten note at top: April 17, 2020 — People who think they are religious but say things they shouldn't are just fooling themselves

Day Twenty-five

James 1:26

If anyone among you thinks he is religious, and does not bridle his tongue but deceives his own heart, this one's religion is useless.

Once a pastor was asked about his parish. "How many members do you have?"

"Just under 1000," he replied.

"How many of your members are active?" he was then asked.

"All my members are active," he answered. "About 100 are active for the Lord. The rest are active for the devil."

Have you thought about your life like that? Whatever is not of faith is sin, so if you're not doing it for God, you are you're doing it for the wrong side! That's an awesome (and somewhat scary) thought to contemplate. Those of us that love God should show Him our love by our obedience. Is this easy? Not on our own.

I have a temper. Not that I'm proud of this, it's just a fact of my life. Whenever I feel like blowing up on someone, I remember a passage I read that was written by a 19th century author I enjoy, Ellen White. "Unless we control our words and our temper, we are slaves to Satan. We are in subjection to him. He leads us captive. All unpleasant, impatient, fretful words are an offering presented to his Satanic Majesty. And it is a costly offering, more costly than any sacrifice we can make for God, for it destroys the peace and happiness of whole families. . ."

An offering to "his Satanic Majesty." That gives me the willies, to use Grandma's phrasing. Can you picture him sitting on his infernal throne, with an evil leer on his face as you blow your top and give him an offering? We really don't have a good reason to be offering him anything! And the good news is you don't have to offer him anything. By the grace of God, we are able to stay on God's side and keep our tempers way in the backgrounds.

An old minister told me a secret: you can't pray and sin at the same time. He has a good point. If we are in communion with God, it's going to be hard to do something wrong. He is with us, He protects us from ourselves and our weaknesses. His grace is sufficient for us. All we need to do is ask Him to be with us. And when greatly tempted to let that nut cutting lanes in traffic and not using turn signals send us into a swearing frenzy, take a deep breath, roll your shoulders back and start talking to God-out loud if you're in the car alone. Tell Him how much that guy irritates you. Then just keep the conversation going until you are out of traffic. The temper will cool, because you've changed your focus from that nut in the blue car to God in the blue sky.

Have you asked Him to lead you on your path today?

> "A silly idea is current that good people do not know what temptation means. This is an obvious lie. Only those who try to resist temptation know how strong it is. . . A man who gives in to temptation after five minutes simply does not know what it would have been like an hour later. That is why bad people, in one sense, know very little about badness. They have lived a sheltered life by always giving in."

> *April 18th 2020*
>
> *From birth, evil people turn away from God, they wander off and tell lies as soon as they are born* – C.S. Lewis

Day Twenty-Six

Psalms 58:3
"The wicked are estranged from the womb; They go astray as soon as they are born, speaking lies."

Would you like to see example of a truly self-centered, egotistical, demanding person? Are you expecting me to say Adolf Hitler or Attila the Hun or Pol Pot or Osama Bin laden or Saddam Hussein or maybe your boss or professor?

Don't be too surprised when I tell you to just take a visit to your nearest hospital and look at all the newborns in the newborn nursery. If there's ever anything so self-centered as a newborn baby, I don't know what it could be.

I can just hear you saying, "Babies are so cute and so helpless and they need their mommy so much, of course, they cry." Well, yes, that is true. But it doesn't matter whether Mom has a cold or Dad has to get up early for work, that baby wants what he wants and he wants it now and he is not taking no for an answer!

Everyone is born sinful; that is, selfish and self-centered. Everyone is born separated from God. People have real trouble with that idea. The thought that a cute little baby could be sinful is hard for them to accept. I know I had trouble with the concept back when I was a young, unmarried (read inexperienced, naïve and hopelessly romantic) engaged person.

No more. You see, I've had kids now. I had six children and I well remember 3 o'clock feedings, constant diapers, being spat-up on at church. I remember kids screaming at their baby dedications and fussing during prayer meeting or demanding to be breast fed while I was trying to do the grocery shopping. I've seen how selfish and sinful people are when they are small. (And sometimes, in my therapy practice, even when they are much older.)

The apostle Paul says in Romans 3, verse 10, "There is none righteous, no, not one."

Have you heard the folktale of the lady and the snake? It was winter and the lady heard a noise on her porch. She opened the door and was horrified to see a large diamondback rattler lying there by the door.

"Let me in," it begged. "I'm freezing to death."

"You'll bite me and I'll die," she said.

But the snake said he wouldn't, he promised he would just come in, get warm, and then she could let him back out. So she let him in to lie by the fire. She gave him some warm soup to lap up. As she was turning to go, he struck her on hand.

"Why did you do that? You promised!"

"I couldn't help it. It's my nature. You knew I was a snake when you let me in."

That's the dilemma we find ourselves in. We have fallen natures. We realize we're destroying ourselves and our planet, but we seem helpless to do anything about it because our problem goes deeper than we can manage. The answer to our problem is deeper than just behavioral changes.

God has to get to our hearts and change them. We must receive new natures, or we will never escape the corruption we have within us. Our sinful tendencies must be destroyed and replaced by new tendencies to do good. Only then can we escape ourselves. Only then can we quit being a snake.

"As the salt flavors every drop in the Atlantic, so does sin affect every atom of our nature. It is so sadly there, so abundantly there, that if you cannot detect it, you are deceived".

Charles H. Spurgeon

1 John 5:10 All who believe in the Son of God know that this is true. Those who don't believe this are actually calling God a liar because they don't believe what God has testified about his son

April 19 2020 1 John 4:10 This is what real love is. It is not our love for God. it is God's love for us in sending his Son to be the way to take away our sins

Day Twenty-Seven

1 John 4:10 *(5)*

He that believeth in the Son of God hath the witness in himself.

Translation is such a strange business. In Japan, there was a sign for Tokyo tourists who were driving for the first time in the crowded Tokyo streets. It read, "When a passenger of the foot heaves into sight, tootle the horn. Trumpet at him melodiously at first, but if he still obstacles your passage, then tootle at him with vigor."

Coca-Cola cans in Japan at one time carried the slogan, "I feel Coke and Sound Special."

The original Pepsi slogan "Pepsi brings you back to life" transposed into Chinese Mandarin came out "Pepsi brings your ancestors back from the grave"

When Parker Pen marketed a ball-point pen in Mexico, its ads were supposed to have read, "It won't leak in your pocket and embarrass you." The company thought that the word "embarazar" (to impregnate) meant to embarrass, so the ad read: "It won't leak in your pocket and make you pregnant."

A hotel in Yugoslavia once warned tourists, "Guests should announce the abandonment of their rooms before 12 o'clock, emptying the room at the latest until 14 o'clock, for use of the room before 15 at the arrival or after 16 o'clock at the departure, will be billed for one night more." Say what?

Translation is a hard business. It is a special skill to make sure one language does not shade the true meaning in another. So people who translate the Scriptures have many problems. How do the Bible translators translate the Bible into the jargon of the people? Even translating English slogans from one language to another can have difficulty with the idiomatic phrasing. But what about one region to another or one culture to another?

What do the Eskimos know about the true vine; where there are no vines? Or the good shepherd where there are no sheep? How do we explain to the aborigines the story of the good Samaritan? Or to people who have no concept of love, God's love? It is, as my mom used to say, a sticky wicket.

I admire the translators. I really do. To try and transpose God's word, not to change its meaning, but to make it meaningful, is a huge gift. To make His grace available to a fallen world that doesn't know of grace is an occupation that God must really work with and bless. But closer to home, what is your translation? Do the people around you see God in your translation? Each of us is a form of Bible. We are witnesses. When people look at you, they see your version of Christianity. Is your translation clear? Can the world see God in you? Or do you fog the windows and screw up the meaning with your actions? Are you kind, as God is kind? Ask God to help your translation of His love today. Let Him speak through you clearly. You may be the only example of His love some people ever come across.

"You are the only Bible some unbelievers will ever read."

John MacArthur

Handwritten note at top: April 20, 2020 — If you use your mouth to say, Jesus is Lord and if you believe in your heart that God raised Jesus from the dead you will be saved. We believe with our hearts, and so we are made right with God. And we use our mouths to say that we believe, and so we are saved.

Day Twenty-eight

Romans 10:9,10

"That if you confess with your mouth the Lord Jesus and believe in your heart that God has raised Him from the dead, you will be saved. For with the heart one believes unto righteousness, and with the mouth confession is made unto salvation."

When I was a kid, my dad used to say that anything made in Japan or China were cheap goods and wouldn't last. That isn't true today, but the government of the 50's allowed a lot of really cheaply made things into the country to help the trade deficit and enable those countries to recover from the destruction caused by war. Those cheaply made goods created a stigma that lasted a long time. It was as if things coming from those countries were an imitation of what was actually needed: shoes that had soles falling off, clothing that shrank with washing, toys that broke before you got them home from the store. People got pretty fed-up with it and it actually ended up working against the countries concerned.

People in our modern society have accepted a different standard now. Almost everything is considered disposable; things go out of fashion and have to be replaced. Did you know that we've known for more than a generation how to make lightbulbs that will last for years; however, they weren't manufactured because the companies would go out of business without returning customers. They make them last just long enough to make you forget when you got them, usually around six months. Then, believing the hype that this or that one is better, you go buy more. Clothing dyes can be made not to fade so you don't have to replace the clothing so often, but it's not economically feasible to let people actually wear out their clothing completely. (I dye yarn made from fibers from my own animals and a good mordant makes the color permanent as can be-your clothing really doesn't have to fade so much from washing.) Computers generally last just about two, possibly three years; cars last almost as long as the loans we take to buy them.

It's all based on economics. Craftsmanship seems to have gone out of fashion, like statesmen in politics. But how many of us have a piece of furniture that belonged to dear old aunt whomever, that still looks beautiful after all these years? I have one of my grandfather's pocket knives that still holds a great edge and works just fine. I got a new pocketknife at Christmas that snapped and broke when I tried to cut twine on a bale of hay.

But one thing stays the same and has been since Creation: God's love. It is not cheap. It is not free of cost to God, but is to us, and if we believe in Him and His Grace and His resurrection, and if we admit our faults to Him and ask His forgiveness, then we are saved by Him.

It is as sure as beautiful antique furniture that has been in the family for years. The craftsmanship of God lasts for eternity.

"Cheap grace is the preaching of forgiveness without requiring repentance, baptism without church discipline, Communion without confession,

absolution without personal confession. Cheap grace is grace without discipleship, grace without the cross, grace without Jesus Christ".
Dietrich Bonhoeffer

Day Twenty-nine

1 Corinthians 10:13
"No temptation has overtaken you that is not common to man. God is faithful, and he will not let you be tempted beyond your ability, but with the temptation he will also provide the way of escape, that you may be able to endure it."

Have you ever had one of those days when you simply wonder how evolutionists could possibly believe in evolution with all the wonderful examples of total silliness we are seemingly surrounded with every day?

Example. I was shopping. My purchase rang up to $21.54. I gave the cashier 22.54. She gave me back the change, told me she had to give me 46 cents because it was company policy not to give back dollar bills because it messed up the cash drawer. What?

A friend of mine told me she was at a meeting with her child's schoolteacher and was asked whether or not it was true her child was a native American? When it was affirmed, the teacher said. "Oh, that explains why he has such trouble with math." (never mind Dr. Robert Meggison, an Oglala Sioux from University of MI who developed Banach spaces or Thomas Storer, Ojibway, professor emeritus of mathematics at UMI, Mary Ross, Cherokee, a founding member of Skunkworks...)

Every time I go into a grocery, I see signs of inanity and wonder who falls for them. For instance, a while back in my local grocery, they had three displays on strawberries in two places. On one display, a pound of strawberries was advertised as $2.25 a pound. On another display, they were two for $5.00. In the last display, two pound boxes were 3.99. so the normal shopper would look, see they were all the same brand, all the same grade, and chose the least expensive, right? No. People grabbed the two for five berries. A two pound box has the same amount of berries a dollar cheaper, yet the stack seemed untouched.

I met a young lady who had died her hair in rainbow colors, then actually taken sharpies and colored her freckles to match. I admire individuality, but for real?
And what about the young men I sometimes deal with who have tattoos on their face, arms, neck, hands? Some of my social worker friends call them "I ain't ever going to get a good job tats." Were they awake when all that happened?

So what is a Christian to do when confronted with out and out foolishness? Don't lose it, remember God wants us to be kind and respectful and not lose our cool over the mundane oddities of life. You see your child with Oreo crumbs on his face, cookies in his hand and he insists the dog did it? Sigh, put the cookie jar higher and remember, to God's eyes we are as children, and He cares for us each and every one. It takes little to be kind, and getting upset over it does no good. Just smile and go on, and praise God for all His wonderful diversity.

"If a man cannot be a Christian in the place he is, he cannot be a Christian anywhere."

Henry Ward Beecher

Day Thirty

Proverbs 3:1-35, selected phrases

My son, do not forget my teaching, but let your heart keep my commandments, for length of days and years of life and peace they will add to you. Let not steadfast love and faithfulness forsake you; bind them around your neck; write them on the tablet of your heart. So you will find favor and good success in the sight of God and man. Trust in the LORD with all your heart, and do not lean on your own understanding.

I have worked with children who have Reactive Attachment Disorder (RAD). In the first three years of their lives, they were not loved. They did not learn to trust or bond to anything, because when they cried, no one came. When they were hungry, no one fed them. When they were dirty, no one cleaned them, so they learned the world is a place to not trust, to not expect help, to have no faith in anything but what is here now, within reach.

It's as if there is a heart shaped black hole in their minds where a memory of love ought to have been formed. They are not capable of empathy. They cannot feel for others. They have a continual need, a want for that which they never got. They are manipulative, unkind, they live for conning others into helping them fill their endless uncertainty about the world. They are incredibly difficult to work with, because building any kind of a trust relationship where change can happen devolves into just teaching them coping skills. Many things have been tried, but RAD is simply not a curable ailment. The brain is permanently damaged by lack of caring.

God does not want this for any of us. When we are born again into His Kingdom, we need to be nurtured, like babies in the faith. We need to be shown love, and learn the culture that will travel with us to heaven. We need to not be ignored and expected to just do what the others do, but to be kept safe and raised into the faith. Too often have I seen people baptized, accept Christ and drop away within a year because the church members felt their job was completed when the water closed over the person's head. In effect, they helped deliver a child in the world and left them to have no one to bond to, no place to call home. We leave them worse off than before because now they will be resistant to the Spirit's leading since they see God in us, and we didn't show them care. We showed them our indifference. We showed them they weren't worth our time. In a sense, we abandoned newborns as if what their lives became after they were saved did not matter. So they catch a form of RAD and they leave quietly and we don't see them again; or if we do, they duck and run. They tell their friends there is nothing to this God stuff. It's all hype and numbers. How it must grieve the heart of God! We need to obey Him and we need to show others how to live by our lives, and that includes bringing them into our lives.

"The Bible is the story of two gardens: Eden and Gethsemane. In the first, Adam took a fall. In the second, Jesus took a stand. In the first, God sought Adam. In the second, Jesus sought God. In Eden, Adam hid from God. In Gethsemane, Jesus emerged from the tomb. In Eden, Satan led Adam to a tree that led to his death. From Gethsemane, Jesus went to a tree that led to our life."

Max Lucado

Day Thirty-one

John 3:16,17

For God so loved the world that He gave His only begotten Son, that whoever believes in Him should not perish but have everlasting life.

For God did not send His Son into the world to condemn the world, but that the world through Him might be saved.

I was talking to a non-believing friend the other day and we got onto the topic of faith and he told me this verse had always stymied him, this John 3:16 that was always being thrown at him like it ought to make sense. I asked him why it didn't to him, of course. He said it was good that people believed that God came to save them and die for them, but why would God condemn them for just being people and send them to an eternally burning pit? Seventy years of maybe messing up here in exchange for burning forever? It didn't seem fair or just at all. Besides, all it takes is just belief and you get out of it? Even the really wicked like Hitler or Bin Laden punished like some poor guy who just never heard about it? What sort of God was that?

Of course I realized, as he'd never really read the Bible, he was being quite honest in this error of thought. It's actually a series of thoughts we'll sort out over the next few days but let's take the main error first. No one had bothered to complete the idea in verse seventeen that is given in the entire sentence; he normally only heard folks quoting verse sixteen, not going on to verse seventeen. God did not send

Jesus in order that He might condemn the world; He never even contemplated "Here He is; someone who actually did it right, so now I can use Him as the eternal standard you must all live up to." No, no, He sent Jesus not to condemn, but as an offering for what we have done. Jesus came to heal our brokenness because we are so far beyond repair that anything less than the actual Creator would not have worked. Jesus is not given us as a way of judgement, but as a way out of judgement. He took our sins that we might take his life record.

I recall a story that happened when the first cars were out on the roads. They weren't always reliable, so men that bought them had to learn how to finagle with them sometimes. One day, a man was at the side of the road. His Ford had stopped. He had checked the petrol; he had checked other things and now he was under the hood trying to figure out what was going on. Another man with his companions stopped to lend a hand and shortly had it up and running. After thanking the gentleman, the man with the now running car handed the repairman his card with a promise that if he could, he'd return the favor. The other man smiled, handed him his card and drove off. The person who fixed the car was Henry Ford, riding along in his Ford. The inventor of the vehicle could repair the vehicle. Since Jesus created us (John 1) he could repair us the best, so He came and He did what was needed to pay for our broken promises. He is the guarantor of the guarantee given us at birth; He will repair us if we allow it.

"When we learn to read the story of Jesus and see it as the story of the love of God, doing for us what we could not do for ourselves – that insight produces, again and again, a sense of astonished gratitude which is very near the heart of authentic Christian experience."

N.T. Wright

April 24 2020 — So give yourselfs completely to God. Stand against the devil, & the devil will run from you.

Day Thirty-Two

James 4:7
Submit yourselves therefore to God. Resist the devil, and he will flee from you.

<u>Satan is a bully</u>. I don't know if you were ever bullied as a child, but I was. My seventh grade in school was incredibly hard. Nothing I ever did was right, nothing I said was cool. I would come home from riding the school bus white faced and shaken by the hatred shown me on the ride. I recall one day in particular was so bad the driver pulled the bus over, moved me to the front and lambasted the entire lot of kids for their cruelty. It was quiet on the way home that day, but they were all back the next morning. I talked to a teacher and she shrugged it off, saying I had to just buck up to it. As long as I got acceptable grades, it was fine. My mom told my dad, and they both felt helpless because back then, there was no other recourse. I lived through eighth grade alone again, and then entered high school where if it were possible, it got worse. The next year my parents sent me away to a boarding school; but for my freshman year, nothing I did helped.

Then my big brother said I needed to fight back. When I was shoved into my locker, shove back. When I was tripped on the stairs, grab them and use them as a cushion. take them down with me. When they called me names, memorize some bad words and give as good as I got. Most of all, find out who the queen bee was who was causing all this pain and plow them down.

153

Now my big brother at this point had graduated and was in the army, heading for Vietnam. He'd lettered in high school, had been fairly popular, so I figured he must know, right? I figured, he made it through high school, he must know what he was talking about. I steeled myself for the next day at school. I thought up the bad words I knew; I didn't know very many but since I read all the time, I had a pretty awesomely large vocabulary. And when I walked into the cafeteria to wait for class, and the usual suspects came over, tried to trip me while I found a seat, laughing at my rummage sale clothes.

I didn't drop everything and fall down like I usually did. I threw the books down, drew back my fist and slammed the first girl in the jaw, the second in the stomach and kicked the third high on her leg and crashed into the fourth. They all went down wailing. I then stood over them with my fists ready and dared them to stand up. I then called them a bunch of "purposeless, monstrously bred, low life cretins, totally, grievously uncouth, nefariously dull-witted with a black hole of soul-destroying, coma-inducing dullness in their everlasting detestably parasitic ways," anyway, you get the main idea. They didn't have a clue what I said and I went on for around two minutes in this fashion. The cafeteria was totally silent. I gathered my books and hiked to the principal's office. I expected to be punished for fighting back. You know what Mr. Larrabee did? He came around to the front of the desk, told me he was glad I stood up to the SOB's and he was giving me a pass this time. When the girls mom's called him-which they did-he would tell them the girls had attacked first and there were enough witnesses to prove it. I couldn't hit anyone else but they didn't have to know that.

And they didn't bother me the rest of that year; which was only two months. I actually made a couple friends among the others who didn't quite fit it.

Would I suggest anyone do that today? Probably not, we're a much more litigatious society. However, the devil is a bully. If you stand up to him, he will go away. When he comes and tries to get you to do something you know the good Lord would not approve of, you can talk back; you can tell him to beat it, and he has to go. You are God's child and he only has access to you when you are not following God's ways. And remember the hint I got from a very old, wise elder I mentioned before?. You can't sin and pray at the same time. The two acts are mutually exclusive. So if you are tempted, start praying to God. The temptation will pass and you will succeed in living the life He wants you to live. And you won't have to go commando and hit people.

"Do all the good you can. By all the means you can. In all the ways you can. In all the places you can. At all the times you can. To all the people you can. As long as ever you can."

John Wesley

Day Thirty-three

Hebrews 13:1-3
Let brotherly love continue. Do not neglect to show hospitality to strangers, for thereby some have entertained angels unawares. Remember those who are in prison, as though in prison with them, and those who are mistreated, since you also are in the body.

I remember as a child when my parents first became Christians and all the changes that happened in our family, it seemed really quickly. From dad giving up booze and cigars, to keeping one day holy, to me ending up in a Christian school, in around six months my world changed.

One day coming home from church we came upon an old man, walking along the highway. Back in those days it was not as dangerous to pick up hitchhikers as now, so dad told Mike to move into the back seat (We had a three bench station wagon), making a place to pick up the old fellow.

Turns out he'd been a farm hand. He'd gotten hurt on the job and after getting back from the ER with his hand all bandaged, he'd found his clothes and such packed into his duffle bag waiting, his final pay in an envelope. He'd been fired for getting hurt on the job. He'd used the paycheck to stay in a cheap hotel for a week until he thought he could use his hand again. Now he was trying to find a farm that could take him on. He'd always been a day laborer. Dad asked him when the last time he'd had anything to eat and he admitted he'd had the last of some cold cereal dry yesterday morning. We took him home. Dad had mom fry up some hamburgers, make some coffee. Dad called around to some of the farmers he knew and got him an interview with a couple local farms. It wasn't harvest season but they'd talk to him at least.

I'd never seen anyone tie into sandwiches like that old man. He was wafer thin, greying hair, clothes worn. Mom packed him a lunch to take with him: Dad slipped some money into the lunch bag and then took him up to the first farm and dropped him off. We never saw him again.

Later that day, dad showed us the verse above; he told us that when you could help someone, you did it. It was something that we were supposed to do. I've never forgotten that lesson. Even in this day of con artists and people who manipulate or could be downright dangerous, I keep some gift cards for local fast food restaurants in my purse and when we see a homeless person, someone in need, we give them a card, try to steer them towards where they can get more help. We've opened our home up a few times to people who needed a bit of help over a bump. Yes, a couple times, we've been taken advantage of, but others times you know this was the right thing to do. God asks of us to be kind, to put ourselves in the other person's place and consider how we'd like to be treated. Someone who needs help, send a prayer up so God can do the screening for you and most times, some food, a place to rest overnight and a hot shower and they will have courage enough to go out and try again. As His people, we aren't only lights-we give off warmth to this cold world as well.

"The essential vice, the utmost evil, is Pride. Unchastity, anger, greed, drunkenness, and all that, are mere fleabites in comparison: it was through Pride that the devil became the devil: Pride leads to every other vice: it is the complete anti-God state of mind."

C.S. Lewis

April 26 2020

Day Thirty-four

John 14:6
Jesus said to him, "I am the way, and the truth, and the life. No one comes to the Father except through me.

How broad is your worldview? I've trained many social workers in my time; I've worked with many more. I find those that cling to their worldview, be it middle class or upper, have a terrible time relating to the people they are serving. They can't make the mental jump from this is how we do it to this is how you see it.

Ruby Payne in her work on classes in American society, defines what she calls the Hidden Rules of Class; it shows how people are taught by the social group they were raised in how to react to the crises and rewards of their world.

For instance, hidden rules for the poor make them not save money because they want instant gratification; nothing is long term for them because if they did save money, relatives would borrow it, and the family is all so they would give it. They depend on each other, on family, to get them through. When they try to get ahead, they can be thought as uppity if they don't give to relatives what the relatives perceive them as having more of than they; so if they save and buy a car, relatives want to either borrow money or the car or both.

The middle class save money because they want to get wealthier, they are concerned by what other people think of them, they need things. The family is not as close knit.

The upper class use money as a tool of control; whoever has the money has the power. Everything is used to make more power. Family bonds are used to accumulate and centralize power.

Enter Jesus, who recognized no classes; he was comfortable talking to the wealthy; he was comfortable living with the poor, he was gentle and admonishing to the middle class. He told us the poor would always be with us, and yet when he saw the widow giving her two mites, said she had given more than any of the wealthy.

When we as Christians follow His leading to help others, we need to check at the door our preconceived notions of what will help a person and treat each one as if they were the only person we're going to work with that day; to treat each one as worthy of respect and each one with mercy and justice, kindness and humility. After all, God owns the universe and all in it, and he treats us that way.

"I realized that all my life, my values were based upon typical middle-class American values: hard work, doing good, living well, owning things, following the rules & being the best I can be… but God clearly says, 'those are not MY values. I value justice, mercy, and humility.'

John Green

April 27 2020

Day Thirty-five

1 Timothy 6:6-10
But godliness with contentment is great gain. For we brought nothing into this world, and it is certain we can carry nothing out. And having food and raiment let us be therewith content.

To be content with what you have in this life surrounded by a culture of gimme, gimme, gimme, is an accomplishment in itself. Like so many begging children we run about wanting a later modeled car, a bigger house we can't care for, more clothes we don't wear, more toys we don't need, all of them wasting the precious minutes of our lives and none of them actually bringing us closer to God and His way of life. I recall one time visiting an older member of our church. She lived all alone in a small 2 bedroom house, she had her garden, she made exquisite quilts. She was 82 at the time and was making peach pies.

They smelled incredible but I asked her if she was expecting company for I teased her a little, surely a little old lady alone couldn't eat four pies. No, she told me, this one is for my son, he'll pick it up after work, and he brought me the peaches so least I could do was make him a pie. This one is for my neighbor three houses down, his wife died a few days ago and I thought it might comfort him to have a homemade pie. And this one is for my neighbor two houses the other way, she 93 and getting up in years and hasn't got much energy for cooking for herself so I make sure she has something hot and tasty at least a couple times a week, so she'll not lose heart. And this one is for us to share while we visit today. I knew you'd come this day, she told me, God always lets me have company on Fridays and I like to be ready when they come.

    Getting up in years sounded odd coming from someone 82 years old, but she was so right. She was content in her life, she was active and helpful and had a reason to be. My son works as a nurse in an old folks' home and he tells heart breaking stories sometimes of folks who are sad, lonely and can't find a reason to be alive anymore since they've been forgotten. Still, in the same facility are people who are sick, weak and never stop smiling. They are content. It is just in how you view your circumstances. It's in your own attitude and response to your life. If you allow the people in advertising to convince you that you must constantly buy things, you will not find happiness. If instead, you use what is given as a wise steward, sharing with others, and showing kindness, you will find the elusive butterfly that is happiness.

    "He who lays up treasures on earth spends his life backing away from his treasures. To him, death is loss. He who lays up treasures in heaven looks forward to eternity; he's moving daily toward his treasures. To him, death is gain."

                              Randy Alcorn

Day Thirty-six

Philippians 4:8-9

Finally, brothers, whatever is true, whatever is honorable, whatever is just, whatever is pure, whatever is lovely, whatever is commendable, if there is any excellence, if there is anything worthy of praise, think about these things. What you have learned and received and heard and seen in me—practice these things, and the God of peace will be with you.

This verse is one my grandma would have called an old time religion verse. Whatsoever things are pure-and she hadn't seen a six o'clock news report on school shootings, since she never had a TV set by choice in her home. She lived a simple life, grew much of their own food, helped her neighbors. What she would have thought of our kids' video games and the violence on the home theater today? She would have been convinced that the world was literally already in hell.

God asks us to hold ourselves to a higher standard than the world, to think on things He would think of, to look at things He could approve of; and I am relatively certain zombies and war games aren't it, nor is rape and kidnapping and school shootings on the news nor are the constant reality shows that seem to just show the worst side of people. I've had kids in my therapy office who were having trouble knowing good from bad; what was wrong about grabbing someone's breasts when the people in the porn dad watched did it and no one cared? How do you keep a moral standard up for the next generation when it appears as if our own has gone the way of model T Fords? Back in the 1800's, a gentleman visiting from France was astonished by the morality of the United States; he said that a woman and her children could safely travel the streets alone with no danger of being accosted, indeed, if in trouble any man would try to aid them. Today, there are places I wouldn't go in broad daylight even with a Pitbull at my side and a concealed carry weapon in my hip holster. (I don't actually own either, but you understand what I am saying.)

Is this what our society has become? Is this what God wanted in the country shining on top of a hill for the world to see? I pray that each of us as Christians will take this to heart and within our own lives, our own families and spheres of influence, drive out anything that keeps us from living the fullest life God has to give. It is no inconvenience to get rid of those things that stress us out, that make us discontented, that encourage anger and tension, which tear our minds from God to take up things which bring us peace and happiness and a closer relationship with the Creator of this world. Is it easy to go against the flow of society and it's norms? No, of course not, but is it not time to do so if for no other reason than our survival?

"Don't quit, and don't give up. The reward is just around the corner. And in times of doubt or times of joy, listen for that still, small voice. Know that God has been there from the beginning—and he will be there until . . . the end.

Joanna Gaines

Day Thirty-seven

James 2:14-24

What good is it, my brothers, if someone says he has faith but does not have works? Can that faith save him? If a brother or sister is poorly clothed and lacking in daily food, and one of you says to them, "Go in peace, be warmed and filled," without giving them the things needed for the body, what good is that? So also faith by itself, if it does not have works, is dead. But someone will say, "You have faith and I have works." Show me your faith apart from your works, and I will show you my faith by my works.

One of my favorite songs/poems, *That's what faith must be* by Michael Card has these words as it's chorus:

> "To hear with my heart
> To see with my soul
> To be guided by a hand I cannot hold
> To trust in a way that I cannot see
> That's what faith must be."

As I write these, I can hear the music going in the back of the mind tunnel that is my memory and I smile as I compare this with Scripture. Do you see a dichotomy in the poem and verse? It really doesn't exist. In one we are told faith without works is dead, being alone; in the other faith is an unseen thing that lives within us, not an action so much as a divine principle.

Can you see how some people would say they don't agree? In the final analysis, faith is the essence of things not seen, and it lives in those of us who live in Christ. The result of that living faith is the love we show others, actual acts of kindness that show just who is leading us on this journey of life. Our lives are the living beacons that others can follow to find their way home. How bright is your light? Can it be seen in your face?

"Sight is not faith, and hearing is not faith, neither is feeling faith; but believing when we neither see, hear, nor feel is faith; and everywhere the Bible tells us our salvation is to be by faith. Therefore we must believe before we feel, and often against our feelings, if we would honor God by our faith."

Hannah Whitall Smith..

Day Thirty-eight

1 Corinthians 13:1-13, selected

Though I speak with the tongues of men and of angels, but have not love, I have become sounding brass or a clanging cymbal. And though I have *the gift of* prophecy, and understand all mysteries and all knowledge, and though I have all faith, so that I could remove mountains, but have not love, I am nothing. And though I bestow all my goods to feed *the poor,* and though I give my body to be burned, but have not love, it profits me nothing. Love suffers long *and* is kind; love does not envy; love does not parade itself, is not [b]puffed up; does not behave rudely, does not seek its own, is not provoked, [c]thinks no evil; does not rejoice in iniquity, but rejoices in the truth; 7 bears all things, believes all things, hopes all things, endures all things.

Love never fails. But whether *there are* prophecies, they will fail; whether *there are* tongues, they will cease; whether *there is* knowledge, it will vanish away. For we know in part and we prophesy in part. But when that which is perfect has come, then that which is in part will be done away.

When I was a child, I spoke as a child, I understood as a child, I thought as a child; but when I became a man, I put away childish things. For now we see in a mirror, dimly, but then face to face. Now I know in part, but then I shall know just as I also am known. And now abide faith, hope, love, these three; but the greatest of these *is* love.

I'm a cancer survivor. During my bout with cancer, deep into my chemotherapy, I discovered some things about love.

Love still loves when your hair has all fallen out; when you're crabby because your gums are bleeding; when you have to do the grocery shopping at 3 am when there are less crowds because your immune system is compromised. Your back goes out when you have surgeries, and going to the chiropractor means the dear man opens his office for you a half hour before the other patients come so you can have your adjustment and not be exposed to germs.

Love is still love when you hurt all over and you can't be touched, when you can't sleep if there are covers over you because they hurt just from the weight of them. You learn to be always too cold or too hot as your temperature fluctuates and you really can't dress in layers because it hurts.

Love doesn't care if you are weepy or when the bills pile up because you can't work for now.

Love goes to battle when someone tries to take your kids away because you are sick; love contacts your friends who are lawyers and able to do something about it. Love is those same lawyers making calls to judges and getting it stopped without your appearance because they are good people.

    Love doesn't care when you can't leave the bathroom because you can't stop throwing up in the sink while sitting on the toilet, leaking at both ends as it were and wrapped in just a towel.

    Love is there. Looks can fail; hair fall out or turn grey, and love is still there. God is love; but so is my husband. I am fortunate because I am the apple of two sets of eyes, divine and human. I am the most fortunate of all people, for I have known love.

    "God loves each of us as if there were only one of us."
Augustine

handwritten: May 1 2020

handwritten: he will forgive our sins because we can trust God to do what is right.

Day Thirty-nine

1 John 1:9
If we confess our sins, he is faithful and just to forgive us our sins and to cleanse us from all unrighteousness.

I thank God for this verse. No matter what I have done, he has covered it; He has gotten rid of all the past. He has made me forgiven in the eyes of the universe. I am able to walk the streets of heaven knowing that I am a forgiven child of God. He is faithful in all His promises and in this promise He has told us that no matter what our sin, He is there to forgive if we confess our error.

No matter what your sin, what your past, come to Him as soon as you realize that you have blown it yet again. Go to a quiet place and apologize as you would your own mom or dad or best friend. Tell Him you are sorry and please fix the broken place, make it new. He has promised to do just that. That thing you did, once given to God, is gone.

I heard a story once of a man who asked God to forgive him of something he had done; God freely forgave. The man came back and said, Lord, you know that thing I confessed the other day? And God answered no, I don't. I forgave, it's gone. Forget it now, because I have. Your sin is as far from me as the east is from the west. That thought that weighed your mind is taken away. He promised. It's forever gone. He doesn't break His word. We are free.

"He is no fool who gives what he cannot keep, to gain what he cannot lose."
                                   Jim Elliot

May 2 2020

Day Forty

John 16:33

"I have said these things to you, that in me you may have peace. In the world you will have tribulation. But take heart; I have overcome the world."

This world we live in is a mess, there are no two ways about it. From abuse, violence and open hostility, to loneliness and fear, from a bumbling economy to new diseases popping up every day, we are simply not doing well.

God knew these times would come. He promised to send us a Comforter to help us through them; and not just through them, but to thrive during the trials we pass.

A Christian comedian was asked what his favorite verse in Scripture might be; he said "This will pass." He said whenever he got worried, upset, frustrated with schedules, he simply remembered that this would be over soon, he just had to take a breath and wait it out. That is an admirable attitude. It's not really Biblical as the phrase used that way doesn't appear in scripture but the idea is a good one.

When something bad happens-it will pass. When someone we loves treats us poorly, or goes away, or dies; it will pass. When you lose your job, this will pass. The immediate problems we have are just a small thing in the overall scope of the world. It hurts now, but think of a month from now, or a week or a year; it will pass.

Tell God about it, ask His help, then leave it. He will give to you what is needed when it is needed. Be patient, let it pass over you. The fire will not burn you; the snake bite will not kill you, the pain will end sometime. For now, let it pass. Keep his peace in your heart, and you can let it pass. The peace that passeth all understanding is not just a saying-it's the truth of the Christian life. We let God take our hurts, our worries, we hand them to Him, and we simply wait in faith knowing that this will pass.

I have many times told clients who were anxious about everything and nothing, worried about what was going to happen, and admitting it almost never did that to talk to God, hand it over to Him is such a relief. You need to be accepting of His answers and sometimes we will not understand them, but the present situation will be gone tomorrow. Your needs will be met, He will give you an idea of what to do and simply do what He suggests and it all comes out. I can't explain it; I have simply seen it happen again and again.

"Life is wasted if we do not grasp the glory of the cross, cherish it for the treasure that it is, and cleave to it as the highest price of every pleasure and the deepest comfort in every pain. What was once foolishness to us—a crucified God—must become our wisdom and our power and our only boast in this world."
John Piper

Day Forty-one

Ezekiel 34:26
And I will make them and the places roundabout my hill a blessing, and I will cause the shower to come down in his season, there shall be showers of blessing.

I heard tell of a man who decided to test God. He thought he did as much for God as God did for him, and he was going to prove it. So he got a ledger book. On the left side he titled the page "What I do for God." On the right-hand page he titled it "What God does for me." He began to write things down. Whenever he felt ill and recovered, he wrote it on God's side. Whenever a special blessing came his way, he put on God's side. When somebody was kind to him unexpectedly, God's side. At the end of the month, he looked at the book. "It's no use," he declared. "I can never get a balance. I am always going to be hopelessly in debt to God."

He was right. If you just take notice of it, God is continually gifting us. His blessings are all around us.

I am fond of telling my children that every Sabbath day, God sends us a surprise and it's up to us to find it. They have never been disappointed; from new kittens in the barn to the first robin of spring, to new flowers to a baby cria-there is always something to be thankful for just on the day when we can stop and enjoy it the most, just to make it special. I recall one time the entire day seemed to go by with nothing too special; it rained, we couldn't go out all day. It was late when the sky cleared and we could go out. The sky cleared, then twilight came, the sky darkened and just then there were three shooting stars crashing, streaking across the sky-it took all day but He didn't let us down.

Too often we think too highly of ourselves. We think He really owes us for being good. Yet if we would just take a little time and write down all the blessings we've had for the week, will be surprised at just how much God does for us. The blessings of health, clear minds, friends and family, even material things like the ability to pay our bills and buy things we need or want are all gifts from God. Just being alive is a gift. There is a story told of Francis of Assisi, the saintly monk who loved all God's creatures. He was asked how he was able to accomplish so much. "Perhaps this is why. The Lord looked down from heaven and said, 'where can I find the weakest, littlest, meanest man on earth' and then he saw me and he said, 'I found him. I will work through him. He won't be proud of it. We'll both see I'm only using him because of his total insignificance.'"

In our family, each Friday evening we write down on slips of paper the blessings we had from last week, and at Thanksgiving, I take them all out, put them in date order, and make a list. We never fail to have three or four single spaced pages of blessings in any year. And as we go back over the list, we remember how we have been led.

We are really so small. His love for us is so great. We are always going to be in his debt to Him for our very lives. Isn't it time we started to give Him the honor and love He so deserves?

"There is no limit to the amount of good you can do if you don't care who gets the credit."

Ronald Reagan

[Handwritten: May 4th 2020 — In the same way, younger people should be willing to be under older people & all of you should be very humble with each other. God is against the proud, but he give grace to the humble]

Day Forty-two

1 Peter 5:5

"likewise, ye younger, submit yourselves unto the elder. All of you be subject one to another, and be clothed with humility, for God resists the proud, and giveth grace to the humble."

"It isn't fair!" Lilia pouted. "I'm big enough to take care of myself. Why can't I go over to Maya's house?"

"She's not good for you," her father said quietly, reading his newspaper.

"And just how is going to her house going to hurt me? Her mom will be there."

"She's not a Christian." Dad turned the page, reading peacefully.

"I'm not doing anything wrong. I just want to talk to her a while."

Her father went over to the fireplace and took out a dead coal. He held it out to Lilia. "Here, take it. It won't burn you."

"It's dirty. That will black my hands all up." Even as she spoke the words, she understood their meaning. Going with bad company will soon change you, too. You know inside when someone is not right to be around. With some people, it's best to be on a name only basis. Some people are downright dangerous. People who do drugs or alcohol, for instance. Some are not so open but they will blacken your mind with doubts and bad language. Keep yourself free of those kind of people. Toxic people bring pain and harm. They poison your mind; they hurt your peace.

Do we stay away and neglect witnessing to them? Of course not, but you can witness to someone without being a best friend. You may show kindness without being involved in their lifestyle. Be peaceful, express God's love, but show discernment and your life will be much better.

"The Bible says we need to love our enemies, bless our enemies. It does not say we should assume our enemies' priorities."

David McGee

Day Forty-three

Isaiah 55:11
My word shall not return to me void.

I read a story about a minister in Charleston, West Virginia, who got a parking ticket. He was visiting a critically ill person in a hospital and overstayed his time on the meter. He came out of the visit and got the notice on his windshield. Thinking it over, he decided to go to court with the ticket.

At the traffic court the judge asked him what took him so long.

"It's like this, your Honor," he replied. "The job of saving the man's soul before he died took longer than I expected. The parking ticket is worth whatever it cost me knowing the man was saved before he died."

The judge thought a moment, smiled, and tore up the ticket. "I agree wholeheartedly," he said. "Peace of mind before you pass away is worth more than a ticket to this city and bringing comfort to the dying is an excusable act. There is no sensible rationale for the ticket. You're excused from the court."

Sometimes, God's times take a little bit longer than you expect. Sometimes you may decide to spend 10 minutes each morning reading your Bible. You get through 1 Corinthians 13 and start to pray. You ask His guidance and you keep remembering friends you need to pray about, and the next thing you know half an hour passes. It happens more often than you might think once you get close to God.

Don't begrudge the time spent with God. It's worth the world to save souls; to pray for your friends is worth the time. You may not know this side of heaven what your prayers have accomplished, but God's service is always rewarded. The joy of heaven is worth the inconvenience of now.

You will feel sometimes an urge to speak to someone, or to do something, and you shake your head and start considering what might happen. You are prompted to speak a word for God to a co-worker, or you notice someone riding on the elevator looks sad and God nudges you and says smile at that person, wish them good day. Little things; but follow those things. God is starting to use you. It's a good thing. You will learn from it. It will strengthen your faith.

"Don't be a fool. Recognize your dependence on God. As the days become dark and the nights become dreary, realize that there is a God who rules above.

Martin Luther King Jr.

May 5th 2020

my son keep your fathers commands + don't forget your mother's teaching

Day Forty-four

Proverbs 6:20
My son, keep thy father's commandment, and forsake not the law of thy mother

I have a calculator. It causes me no end of trouble. You see, if I don't poke in the right numbers, it won't give me the right answer. That' s unreasonable. It's supposed to be a help and all it does is give me wrong answers. I bought it to help me balance my checkbook, and it just told me I am $2, 590.87 overdrawn. Of course, I neglected to tell it where to put the decimal and I forgot to tell it the about the deposit I made at the bank this morning but it was in my pocket at the bank with me and it ought to pay attention when I go to the trouble of carrying it around.

Am I being facetious? Yes, of course I am. The machine can only do what I tell it to do. If I want it to give me right answers I have to give it the right numbers to calculate. It cannot see or hear or learn from watching me. Do you know anyone like the person I'm describing?

I know some children who act that way to their families. They expect mother to know when they have torn their pants even if they've stuffed them under the bed and forgot to tell her about them. I have seen boys who just knew their dad knew he was supposed to go to the program with them tonight. Never mind that they forgot to give him the note from their teacher about it. These kids think their big sisters should know what they did with their shoes as if all sister has to do is pay attention to where they drop things. In short, hey think the world must revolve around them. They don't take care of themselves and they expect others to do their work for them.

It's bad enough in younger kids but have you met adults who feel entitled? I recall talking to one such young fellow who could not believe he'd been fired at work. His problem wasn't drugs, or alcohol, or tardiness or absenteeism. He couldn't stop checking his phone on the job. It seemed like every time the foreman walked by, he had it out, looking to his job with one hand, looking at the screen with his eyes. It was too dangerous to keep him on the line. And he was in my office wanting me, the shrink, to write him a note to his job to get him back his job. I blinked a few times over that one.

We recently had a case in our town where two little kids, ages 2 and 3 were found wandering down the middle of a city street in diapers. When the police went door to door, they found the mom deeply in a conversation with a friend on skype-she didn't even know they'd "escaped" out the back door. She thought they were taking naps. Worse, when she was brought up on neglect charges, she didn't blame herself, she blamed the babies. When did taking responsibility for our own actions become so unfashionable?

So what do we do as Christians? Do we expect the minister to do all the work at church, or the praise team or the paid staff? Do we expect the gospel to spread itself?

In this little book, we've been trying to acquire a God Habit-and one of the things we need to recognize is God takes this seriously and He just might expect you to find ways of giving service to others and take responsibility for our own actions. Just because someone else is acting entitled does not mean it's a good thing. Once you and God have a clear channel of caring back and forth, you can expect Him to expect you to begin working in His field with Him- as He told Peter "feed my Sheep." We are all responsible for ourselves and for others.

"The time is always right to do what is right"
Martin Luther King, Jr.

May 2020 — I mean that you have been saved by grace through believing. You did not save yourself & it was a gift from God.

Day Forty-five

Ephesians 2:8,9

For by grace you have been saved through faith, and that not of yourselves; it is the gift of God, not of works, lest anyone should boast.

I remember my son as a small boy coming in from a long morning outside with his dad and proudly announcing that he had just finished cultivating the garden. And looking at my husband, knowing the little guy couldn't possibly have been running the rototiller in the garden. Dan smiled and said, "He picked up sticks for me and put them on the pile. He was a big help."

Now knowing I had already gone over the garden the night before to get it ready for tilling, I realized my 6 year old really hadn't done much. However, he did want the credit for doing it.

Isn't that just like us? Salvation is a free gift of God. We can't even pick up the sticks of our lives by ourselves. But we stubbornly refuse to believe we can't do *something*! Yet it is a complete and honest gift, no cost to us, no bill to pay – He just wants our love, acceptance and gratitude for the suffering He had to go through to wrap it up and give it to us.

There is no way we can pretty ourselves up by ourselves and make ourselves into what we aren't – perfect and clean – before we come to Him and ask for the gift. We come as we are: weak, full of errors and anger, full of sorrow and sadness, and we ask Him to cover us up, please, and make us acceptable to the watching universe. And He does it!

I don't understand how it works completely; I don't think anyone does, but somehow He covers us and we become, in the eyes of the universe and God, like a mirror image of Him. We are loved at once, accepted at once, cared for and treated as a precious child of the king, just for asking and believing what He promised. What an amazing thing is salvation! God is so good, all the time!

"Why do we act as though our sin disqualifies us from the grace of God? That is the only thing that qualifies us! Anything else is a self-righteous attempt to earn God's grace. You cannot trust God's grace 99 percent. It's all or nothing. The problem, as I pointed out earlier, is that we want partial credit for our salvation. We want to be 1 percent of the equation. But if we try to save ourselves, we forfeit the salvation that comes from Jesus Christ alone, by grace through faith."

Mark Batterson

Day Forty Six

Genesis 3:6
So when the woman saw that the tree was good for food, that it was pleasant to the eyes, and a tree desirable to make one wise, she took of its fruit and ate. She also gave to her husband with her, and he ate.

Did Eve fall because she ate the apple? Or did she eat the apple because she was fallen? There's a world of difference.

In fact, she fell long before she ate the apple. Taking the apple was just the outward appearance of the inner life. Eve mistrusted God, and that mistrust led to her fall. The Bible says "charm is deceitful and beauty is passing, but a woman who fears the Lord, she shall be praised." (Proverbs 31:30) When Solomon, who wrote most of Proverbs, started depending on his own wisdom, he fell and his God-given wisdom abandoned him. (How do you explain 1000 wives and concubines?)

Do you do sinful things? How about "little" wrong ones – do you lie on your income taxes, do you go just over the speed limit, do you cut corners on projects? Do all these little sins make you sinful? No, you are sinful, so you do these things. The sin in your life shows itself by sinful actions. The spiritual state of your soul can be seen by your actions. That's why so many people are prone to quote Matthew 7:15, "You will know them by their fruits."

Let's look at an example in nature. (I think nature is God's second book, and I learn much by watching, observing and listening to nature.)

Paradise whydah: even the name sounds special. They are such beautiful birds, at least during mating season. I had a pair once. During mating season, the male grows a tail nearly 3 feet long of wide, black-purple, iridescent feathers. His regular bland, beige plumage turns a brilliant rust and white and black. It all shimmers, iridescent blue, green black purple; he is eye-catchingly gorgeous and he knows it. The female doesn't grow the tail he does, but she's impressed with his. They spend long happy afternoons singing to each other and showing off. But that's where the niceness ends.

Paradise whydahs are parasites, pure and simple. They are lazy and they can't be bothered to care for their own eggs. The female looks for the nest of a fire finch, a lovely little bright red bird. She waits until the finch goes to find food, then lays her eggs in its' nest and merrily flies off to sing by her mate while the poor little fire finch has to raise the whydah's babies. The finch raises the extra baby right along with hers, never realizing she has a freeloader on her hands. The babies are similar in size and color at first, but the intruder gradually shoves the real finches out of the nest . The fire finch doesn't know anything until the whydah grows bigger than the others and flies away.

My grandma had a saying, "pretty is as pretty does". The whydah is a pretty bird but she's lazy. Her disposition does not match her looks.

Are you like a whydah? Are you more concerned with preening and playing and being nice to look at than helping others? Do you hide your sins with a pretty veneer so that you think people can't see it? Some folks can put on a good front for a while, but the real problem is in their hearts. And they know, in their hearts, they have problem.

That problem is sin. The only way to get rid of sin is to get to know Jesus. As we know him, He takes away sin and He replaces it with good things. You aren't empty ever. He fills you with peace, love, joy, more than you would ever consider yourself capable of having in your life. You just need to get closer to him and he will take care of your sin problem.

"To confess your sins to God is not to tell [God] anything [God] doesn't already know. Until you confess them, however, they are the abyss between you. When you confess them, they become the bridge."   CS Lewis

People To Help You Maintain Change

Outstanding people, whose lives have shown and taught us grace and dignity, integrity and caring are worth thinking about on our trip.

The next part of our path to travel with God is to meet some of His other servants. Someday, when we all get to heaven, look them up and spend a quiet afternoon with them. They'll be worth talking to and learning about.

And just to let you know, I won't be putting the prayer guide on for you to fill in each day now; it's time you graduated to a prayer journal. You're growing in your relationship and this is yet another tool you can learn to use.

You know now what basic prayer is like and undoubtedly are finding prayer a little easier now, so I am suggesting from here you use the pages near the back of the book to write your specific requests down and when those requests are answered, the answer and the date of your requests. I have never known Him to not answer; not always yes, sometimes a no, but always there is a an answer.

For example, when I was little, my mom had a baby, my sister. I was not allowed to play with the baby and I didn't think it was fair. I was four. I asked God to send me a baby to play with: He probably smiled and I didn't get a baby. Good thing, yes? However, twenty years later, I was married and I got the baby. She's a lovely young lady that I prayed for when I was four, and she was well worth the wait.

I have seen answers so many times, I have prayer journals I've kept over the years full of answers. When I'm down or sad or needing a shot of God inspiration, I get the journals out and look at all the answers over the years: they're well into the hundreds now. Put a marker in page 338 of this book. Start writing down and trusting God to answer you.

I have placed little bullets at the beginning of each line-you can color them or each time there's an answer, add a star sticker to yes's, a happy face sticker for no. That way, as you leaf through these pages, you can see where God has led. Once you've completed this book, you might want to buy a pretty journal to use for the same purpose and set it up the same way-I think I have 10 or more of them now, each with prayers answered showing as shiny stars in my little section of the universe. God bless you as you start remembering how He has answered you.

May 9th 2020

Day Forty-Seven

Isaiah 26:3-4
You will keep in perfect peace all who trust in you, all whose thoughts are fixed on you! Trust in the LORD always, for the LORD God is the eternal Rock.

The great missionary and Adoniarm Judson lay dying. He'd spent his life among the people of Burma. The authorities had put him into jungle prison many times and now his body was failing him. He received a letter telling him that because of his work and his suffering in Burma, Jews in Turkey were being saved through the published account of his trials and pain.

The dying missionary said to his wife, "Love, this awes me."

"Dear, whatever do you mean?" she replied.

"When I was a young man, I prayed to be sent to Jerusalem as a missionary to the Jews. Instead, He sent me to Burma, where I've had a hard life work. But I have always prayed for God's lost people. What awes me is this. I never prayed for anything that He has not answered me, perhaps by the last way imaginable but the answer always came. I have prayed and worked for the Jews, all these years, and I never knew it. The Jews in Turkey were being saved because I worked here. He answered my prayers again." He died shortly after, knowing that his life had been well worth the difficulties.

God always answers prayer. It may not be the one way we expect, but He'll always work out some answer for His children. Once a man who was a scoffer, said to an older lady. "You believe in prayer? Oh well, I need $50. I better go pray for it."

"If you met President Trump this afternoon, would you come right out and ask him for $50?"

The man admitted he probably wouldn't.

"Well then, you'll need to know my heavenly Father a lot better than you do now before he'll give you $50 just for asking."

She had a good point. We need to know God far better than we do in order for him to be able to work with us and for us. If it seems like God isn't answering your prayers, maybe you need to spend more time in prayer getting to know him. First comes the relationship. Then once you know Him, you will know how to pray for the things you really need. You will learn to differentiate between needs and wants. Like any good parent He provides for needs and also for wants but in the proportions that are best for us.

" Our greatest fear should not be of failure but of succeeding at things in life that don't really matter."
Francis Chan

Now turn to **page 338** and write down your requests, pray with Him about them and watch how quickly the answers come! It may be yes, no or wait, but He is faithful.

May 10 2020
Mothers Day

Day Forty-Eight

John 16:33
"I have said these things to you, that in me you may have peace. In the world you will have tribulation. But take heart; I have overcome the world."

The riots in LA were terrible. I remember them like they were yesterday. But out of the terror and that destruction one story stays uppermost in my mind, the story of a black man, a man called Benny Newton.

Benny was the pastor of the Light of Love church. He was listening to the radio as the first reports of the riots began. With a prayer for his people, he drove home to his family. When he got there, his wife had the TV on. The scenes portrayed were sickening. A white man had been pulled out of his truck and was being beaten to death. There were no police anywhere in the picture. He took a deep breath and ran for his clerical collar and his Bible. His wife knew what he was going to do and held Benny just a minute. "My prayers are with you, Benny," she sighed softly. Then he left to try and save the white man at the intersection of Florence and Normandy.

He gunned his old blue Dodge through the intersections. He could see fires starting all around him. He's saw all the gang members with clubs breaking windows and overturning cars. He saw the fury of the crowd and heard the helicopters overhead, the men in the helicopters powerless to do anything except watch. He prayed again, and he felt a sense of calm as the words came out like a whisper in his ear, "Perfect love casts out fear." He got out and began to talk to the crowd. "Brothers! This is not the way. There is another way!"

"Go preach somewhere else, preacher man. You ain't welcome here." The crowd didn't want to listen. One person came at him with a steel bar but when Benny stared him down, he dropped it and ran.

Benny saw a Hispanic man in a pickup truck. His name was Fidel Lopez, and he was trying to get home from work. He looked at everything with fear in his eyes. Gang members bashed in his windshield. The mob rushed the truck, pulling him out, beating him. "I haven't done anything!" He screamed. "What are you doing?"

Benny ran to the rioters. "Stop! Brothers stop!"

"Get out, preacher man. We're showing this spick how Rodney King felt."

Lopez tried to get up to run but was beaten down. Then Benny threw his body over the man. "No more! If you kill him, you kill me!" The mob backed off. He could feel no breath in Lopez's body. "Dear God save him!" he cried.

Nobody stopped to help Benny. Hours passed as Benny stood guard over that man. The rioters moved to another block to terrorize. Another minister came and help

Benny put Lopez into his old Dodge. He took him to Lopez's home where his wife met them. They called an ambulance. It would not come into the area. He tried again. Ambulances were being fired upon and none would come into the area. They took Lopez back out to the old Dodge and drove it to the hospital.

Benny says he stood in the emergency room trying to comfort people who were victims of the riots, and the words came to his head, "Rescue those who are being led to death, hold back those staggering away to slaughter. If you say, but we knew nothing of this, does not he who weighs the heart perceive it? Will he not repay each person according to what he has done?"

This man's brave action in the face of the mob saved a life. One day you may be faced with a decision to help someone in need or turn away to save yourself. Pray that you have the courage to rescue another. Don't be like the priests and the Levites in the Samaritan story. Remember Benny Newton. Pray for the courage to do what is right and then do it.

"Life is wasted if we do not grasp the glory of the cross, cherish it for the treasure that it is, and cleave to it as the highest price of every pleasure and the deepest comfort in every pain. What was once foolishness to us—a crucified God—must become our wisdom and our power and our only boast in this world."

John Piper

May 11th 2020

Day Forty-nine

Isaiah 41:10
Fear not, for I am with you; be not dismayed, for I am your God; I will strengthen you, I will help you, I will uphold you with my righteous right hand.

It was an uprising, such as was common in China in the last century. Someone started a rumor, that started anger, that started riots and suddenly, the countryside was on fire with mobs, attacking anything and anyone they perceived as being involved. One such person, Melissa Monson, was a missionary from England.

Chinese Christians were being killed all over the city as traitors. Bandits and looters took it upon themselves to punish foreigners and their workers as disloyal. Hundreds of Christian Chinese people came to the mission compound in hopes of finding safety. Miss Monson was in bed with an attack of malaria. In her weak state, she was harassed by the devil with temptations. "What will you do when the looters come here? What will you do when the bandits come? Where is your God now?"

Miss Monson began to pray. "Lord, I have been teaching these dear folks about your love. I told them your promises were true. Lord, if your promises fail, all your work here will be in vain. God help us!"

Feeling stronger, she got up to work. All night and the next night she worked among the refugees, helping the injured, keeping their spirits up. They could hear guns all around the mission station. The screams and cries of the tortured surrounded them. Yet the leaders of the bandits never came near the mission compound.

In the morning of the third day, when things were quiet again, people came to the mission asking, "Who are those four shining people, three sitting, one standing, who stood watching from your roof all night?" When told there was nobody on the roof, they refused to believe for they had seen the tall shining ones with their own eyes. This gave Miss Monson an opening to tell about God and his angel guardians. God protects his people, and he protects his work.

Today, the church is under siege from those within who would tear down all God has given us. Do you think he will stand by and do nothing as the criticism and innuendo mounts? There will be a day of reckoning. His church is his best beloved, the apple of his eye, and He will protect it.

"God never said that the journey would be easy, but He did say that the arrival would be worthwhile"

Max Lucado

Day Fifty

Proverbs 16:7
When a man's ways please the Lord, he makes even his enemies to be at peace with him.

Once there was a great statesman named Daniel Webster. One summer he went to his little hometown in New Hampshire for a rest. While he was there, he never missed going to a little country church for services. His niece noticed this and asked him why he would go to hear an old country bumpkin preacher but when in Washington, did not attend the fine Washington church with its highly educated minister. Daniel smiled at her a minute and is reported to have said, "The preacher in Washington preaches to Daniel Webster, the statesman, but this preacher preaches to Daniel Webster the sinner and tells him about Jesus Christ, the Savior." He well understood the power of privilege.

Is it right to act differently to different people, maybe friendly as a puppy to the son of the doctor who drives a BMW but rather short to the young man who walks to school? Yes, I know there's a time and a place for special manners. But as Christians, how should we treat those around us?

For example, if you met an ambassador, did you know you're supposed to address him as your Excellency? However, if you tried calling your pastor, "Your Excellency," he'd think you'd slipped a cog upstairs. It may seem old fashioned to call someone by their surname instead of being on a first name basis with everyone. Yet in all things, we are to make others comfortable and some may not be all that at ease with the familiarity of not calling them Mr. or Miss. You can treat people as an equal without making them feel disrespected.

There is a time to err on the side of etiquette. Do you remember the elder priest Nicodemus who came to Jesus by night to talk as he didn't want anyone to see him? Jesus didn't call him out on it. He was polite and friendly and treated Nicodemus kindly. Later, Nicodemus became a follower and helper to the early church. You remember the tax collector that was so short he had to climb a tree in order to see Jesus? Zacchaeus was called down out of the tree in front of the crowd and told he would be hosting Jesus that day, raising his place in society. Jesus did not condone what the man did for a living, but he treated him kindly and a soul was saved that day.

There is a time and place for respect. There is a time for standing on principle. But among your peers, your friends in the church or the school or work, all need to be treated as an equal. I'm not saying we should not be respectful. It's just that we should be respectful to everybody, not just those who are well-to-do.

"Be faithful in small things because it is in them that your strength lies."

                                                      Mother Teresa

May 13th 2020

Day Fifty-one

Proverbs 22:29
Do you see a man skillful in his work? He will stand before kings; he will not stand before obscure men.

Captains in the Army don't do floors or windows. But Capt. William Pagonis did once and the story bears repeating.

You see, a long time ago, the captain started learning how to work in his father's restaurant as a shoeshine boy. He was 6 at the time and he did a good job. If he didn't, he did the shoes over! He worked his way up in the business with his folks. And when he grew up, his ability to work hard, be on time and polite to all people helped him greatly.

He joined the Army. He worked hard and was promoted all the way to Captain. He was so proud when he came home to show his folks. Back home at the restaurant, the janitor had a night off, so his dad asked him to clean the restaurant after the patrons had left. Captain Pagonis scrubbed the floor and cleaned up the restaurant. You see at home, he wasn't the captain. He was a beloved son.

Pagonis learned early that loyalty to your team is important. Everyone in the family helped each other so they could all make the restaurant a success and support the family. Later, as a lieutenant general in operation Desert

Storm, he earned his 3rd General's star for directing the supply of US troops and supplies to the front. He learned as a child the importance of hard work, cooperation and loyalty and he was a success. So remember that the small jobs you do today are the stepping stones to what you will build up to do tomorrow. Don't shirk your job; be an example of conscientiousness. The world will see you as an ethical person.

And when you speak for Him, speak tall. You are in God's army and you are an ambassador. Get your hands dirty if it gives you a chance to speak about the One we love. He got His hands bloody for us…

"A Bible that is falling apart usually belongs to someone who isn't."

Charles Spurgeon

Day Fifty-two

John 16:22
So also you have sorrow now, but I will see you again, and your hearts will rejoice, and no one will take your joy from you.

Elie was born in Romania in 1928. He had a happy home. With his sisters and brothers he loved going to Hebrew school to learn wisdom from the rabbis. He might've had a simple life but then one man came into his country, in fact, into nearly all of Europe and everything seemed to change overnight.

That man was Adolf Hitler. Hitler hated Jews. He thought all Jews should be killed. Ellie's family like so many other peaceful Jewish people were taken to Buchenwald, a death camp. He was separated from his mother and sisters. His father died. He didn't know from day to day if he would live. The Germans killed so many every day. They gassed them. They worked them hard; they starved them to death. Ellie worked as hard as a boy could. He was just days away from being exterminated. When the United States came and rescued the people at Buchenwald he was only 17 but the scars would stay with him all his life.

He went to Paris to write and start over. After that he went to the United States but his memories haunted him. For 10 years he thought about what happened. He decided to write a book and he called it "Night". He re applied the word "Holocaust" to describe what happened to his people and others who had gone through mass destruction. He authored 57 books, written mostly in French and English. He was a professor, a political activist and a survivor.

While walking in New York he was hit by a taxi in 1956. He had to spend a year in a wheelchair. He was impressed by the kindness of the American people and decided to become a US citizen. He traveled to the Soviet Union to talk to Jews living there and learn about their lives now. His writings are famous. He married another survivor of the Holocaust in 1969 and they have a son. They lived quietly in New York. He lectured and wrote about his experiences. He won several awards, including the Congressional Gold Medal Of Lifetime Achievement. and the Presidential Medal of Freedom.

Eli Weisel won the Nobel Peace Prize in 1986. In his acceptance speech he said, "Let us remember for their sakes and ours. Memory may be our only answer, our only hope to save the world from the ultimate punishment, nuclear holocaust. Anyone who does not remember, betrays them all again." We can never fully understand the pain Elie and others like him have gone through, but we can remember that pain and do everything in our power to see it never, never happens again.

Some of my favorite ideas from Dr. Wiesel are these, well worth pondering:

"We must always take sides. Neutrality helps the oppressor, never the victim. Silence encourages the tormentor, never the tormented.

The opposite of love is not hate, it's indifference.

There may be times when we are powerless to prevent injustice, but there must never be a time when we fail to protest."

On this trip we are taking, it is well worth our time to consider his ideas. The opposite of love is indifference; to do nothing when you know what is right to do is wrong. If you know what you ought to be doing to help someone else and you don't do it, even on a small scale, you miss the opportunity for service and for growing closer to He who always serves us; who gives us life itself.

Elie Wiesel died in New York in 2016. May we all be as dedicated to good as this one man. Would not the world be a safer and kinder place if we took this man's ideas more to heart?

"I'm not afraid of the devil. The devil can handle me – he's got judo I never heard of. But he can't handle the One to whom I'm joined; he can't handle the One to whom I'm united; he can't handle the One whose nature dwells in my nature."
A.W. Tozer

Prayer suggestion: should you ask God to point out to you where you can do the most good today?

Day Fifty-three

Psalm 118:24
"This is the day that the Lord has made; let us rejoice and be glad in it."

"Jackie, can't you just run your little makeup business and be happy? Why do you have to enter these contests? You'll get hurt. You're really successful at your makeup business. You've been businesswomen of the year twice. Isn't that enough?"

"Don't you ever wonder what it's like to go really fast? It must be the most free feeling in the world. I just got to try it," smiled Jackie to her friend. "Hand me that helmet."

Jacqueline Cochran was born in Florida sometime in 1906. Although she claimed to have been an orphan, she actually was the child of a millwright. Her family moved a lot . She had few friends and missed a lot of school. She had less than a third grade education when she quit. She worked from the time she was small. She thought that someday she was going to have everything she wanted. And she dreamed big.

She wanted to fly but she couldn't pass the written exam since she couldn't read. So she taught herself to read. She passed the exam.

In 1932 she got her pilot's license. It took her 3 weeks. Not many people flew in 1932, especially not women. She worked as a salesperson in stores. She saw how cosmetics and permanent waves were harsh on people's skin. She knew there must be gentler potions out there to use. She had taught herself to read and now she began to study the chemistry of cosmetics. She figured out how to do accounting and studied all there was to know about setting up a business. When she was ready, she began Cochran cosmetics. Her nice smelling, gentle creams and lotions were very popular. She was on her way to having everything she wanted.

In 1939 she entered a flying contest and set a new woman's national altitude record. One year later, she broke the 2000 K international speed record. Records fell on a regular basis in front of her. Nobody seem to be able to slow this woman down. Then the war came. She volunteered and with her business acumen and talent, she was made head of the Women's Air Force.

She was the first woman to fly a bomber over the ocean. She received the distinguished service medal in 1945. After training with Chuck Yeager, she became the first woman to break the sound barrier in 1953. In 1962, she was the first woman to pilot a jet over the ocean, in fact, the first pilot of either sex.

Between 1962 and 1964 she established 69 intercity speed records, 9 international speed, distance, and altitude records. In 1969 she was awarded the Distinguished Service Cross for her work with the government. In 1971, she became the first woman to be entered in the aviation Hall of Fame.

She died in 1980 but at the time of her death, she held more speed, altitude and distance records than any man or woman in history up to that point. She proved that anybody can conquer anything they have the desire to work for and beat. Jacqueline Cochran, a homeschooled hero who would not let anything slow her down; be it glass ceilings, invisible boundaries or men who thought she should just make her pretty creams and stay home.

"God has a purpose behind every problem. He uses circumstances to develop our character. In fact, he depends more on circumstances to make us like Jesus than he depends on our reading the Bible."

Rick Warren

May 14 2020

Something from the Spirit can be seen in each person, for the common Good

Day Fifty-four

1 Corinthians 12:7
"But the manifestation of the Spirit is given to every man to profit withal. "

Perhaps someday soon, some of you will be thinking about what you want to be when you get out of school or finish with the present job or just what your next life choice ought to be. This next story may help you figure that out.. Let me tell you a story about one man's and his gifts.

One day, early in his career, Dr. C. Everett Coop was on call at his hospital. He received a beep, called back and was told to come at once: a newborn was in trouble; it could barely breathe and he had to come at once. He broke speed limits to get there in time. The elevators weren't working, so he ran up to the ninth floor to find a small blue baby in an incubator, unable to breathe and dying, lying there in the nursery. He had no time for strict sterile procedure. He laid the baby out on a table and cut open its chest to get at its heart, massaging it to beat again. He performed a special operation right on that table to repair the baby's lungs. He did everything he could to save that child. With a prayer in his heart, he went back to his office. The child's regular pediatrician took over his care, and he never found out whether the surgery had been successful. It was day in the life of an emergency care surgeon.

Twenty-five years later, when he was a respected authority in his field of pediatric surgery, the secretary brought a young man into his office to meet him.

"My father thought you'd like to meet me," he said shyly. "You see, you operated on me twenty-five years ago today, my birthday, when I was only half an hour old. I just completed college and I'm headed for a master's next." Coop's mouth dropped open. With tears in his eyes, Coop ran around the desk to hug the over six foot tall young man. He finally heard the rest of the story of that baby, and he was delighted.

It must be the most wonderful feeling in the world to save a life like that. Yet all around us, people are dying of terminal disease. They die of it every day, and most of us do nothing to save them. The disease is called sin. The cure is Christ. The gifts you been given to use in this life; your time, your talents, are to be used to save people from this disease. You are the doctors and the nurses of God's hospital. You must administer the prescription for God's cure. You have to tell them the story of Christ. You are responsible for your friends and family and everyone that you have in your own circle of contacts. Will you join the on call team, speaking in season, out of season of the cure for sin? Won't you use your gifts to bring them to Jesus, the only cure? You'll save lives. It's why you are here.

After all, it's what His people do because it's what He did when He was here. To follow the Savior is to follow His actions and His teachings and share them when you can. No matter if in secular life you're a waitress or nurse, an engineer or a farmer, a doctor or a teacher, a factory person or a cop walking a beat, you are responsible for the people that you meet. Show them a smile, listen for the urge of the Spirit. Sometimes, you just smile; other times they'll be a little nudge inside that says "this one. Talk to this one." It's your invitation to emergency service.

"The measure of a Christian is not in the height of his grasp but in the depth of his love."
Clarence Jordan

Day Fifty-five

James 1:5
"If any man lack wisdom, let him ask of God, who giveth to all men liberally, and upbraided not."

"Leo, you have got to be crazy! These kids can't possibly succeed. They're migrants, here today, gone tomorrow. Don't waste your time." But Leo didn't listen. He threw himself into developing a way to help the mostly Spanish-speaking students to become adept at math; not just adept, conquerors. After all, if math is a universal language, it ought not matter if you couldn't yet speak English well, you ought to be able to grasp the concepts. And today, 40 years after he started, Leo Ramirez' kids are wizards -- math wizards. In his autobiography, <u>The Wizard Maker,</u> Leo tells us his story and the story of several of his students and frankly, it's amazing.

At age six, math genius Leo Armando Ramirez Sr. knew that he wanted to help others. Reared in the Lower Rio Grande Valley of South Texas among poor hardworking Latino and Hispanic migrant workers, he came to associate education with a better life. He felt led to become a teacher. For thirty-two years, "Mr. Ram" inspired McAllen High School students to reach for more, to push themselves, and to put in their best efforts. The results speak for themselves: under his spell, the McHi Math Wizards captured twenty team state math championships.

His kids have won over a million dollars in math scholarships. They go to ivy league universities and they work for big corporations.

Leo could've believed, like everybody else, that migrant farm worker kids could not learn. They move around so much, following the crops, they aren't in one place long enough to excel at anything. He could've believed that being Spanish and not speaking English could stop anyone; but he didn't. He believed in kids. And those kids caught his fervor and began to believe in themselves. Maybe yes, just maybe this crazy math teacher was right. They conquered because he had faith in them.

Do you need wisdom? God promises to give you what you need if you ask for it and are faithful to him. Will He just magically flip a switch in there and suddenly you speak five languages or all at once calculus becomes clear? No, not normally, although there was that time in Jerusalem when everyone heard in their own language as Peter spoke from the steps of the temple. If it's needed, that sort of miracle it happens. Usually, He helps you with the patience to work, and the wisdom comes as you work. He helps you remember what you're working so hard on and you find you recall better, and it comes easier as you work at it.

I never thought I'd make it through statistics class, a required class in my major. Everyone I'd talked to had gotten tutors for it; they had all broken into study groups, and I was not. I was a forty something returning student and all of them were nineteen or twenty, kids out of high school, just wanting to make their parents happy with their grades so they could stay in school. I had four kids I needed to support and a dream of doing something bigger with my life and a professor who was trying to weed out those he thought were unfit to be here. He had already told me I couldn't succeed. So stats was a big hurdle. Every time I sat down to study, I prayed that the means and medians and ratio definitions would stay where they needed to be. It was not easy. But night by night, I did not give up, and I prayed for the wisdom to sort it out and it did. I ended up acing the course with no tutor to help, no special study group-just stubbornness, prayer and a dream of where I wanted to be in five years…the professor who had predicted I could not stay the course and this class would end it was shown to be wrong. I graduated with honors.

Do you have faith? The kind that can move mountains of prejudice and hate? You need it in this world. And the good news is that you can have it for free; it's a gift. All you have to do is accept that gift, and it's yours. What are you waiting for? You have a world to conquer and you do it on your knees.

"We are all woven together in the great web of humanity, and whatever we can do to benefit and uplift others will reflect in blessing upon ourselves."
Ellen G. White

Day Fifty-six

John 12:26
"If any man serve me, let him follow me, and where I am there shall also my servant be, if any man serve me, him will my father honor."

He stood by his father's coffin. He looked at his Olympic gold medal for a moment, then put it in his father's dead hands. His mother look shocked, but Carl smiled. "Don't worry, mom. This one was for dad. I'll get another one for me."

He went to the Olympics to do just that. In the 100 meter race at the 1988 games, Carl competed against another athlete named Ben Johnson from Canada. Hard as he could, he tried to catch Johnson. But he crossed the line second behind Ben. "It's over, dad," he thought to himself sadly. Johnson made an obscene gesture at Carl, yet Carl was remained a Christian gentleman and good example of sportsmanship..

He just stood a little straighter and shook Ben's hand. He noticed the yellow tinged eyes and the bulging muscles indicating steroid use. "I didn't have the metal, but I could still give to my father by acting with class and dignity." Carl said later.

Straight backed he left the field. Then came the announcement that Johnson had tested positive for steroids and was disqualified from the race. The gold went to Lewis. It was the replacement for the one he had buried with his father. Better yet, he was vindicated.

He earned nine Olympic golds over the years, was named International Sportsman of the Century, and after he retired, went on to become an actor, start a company and run for Senator.

Carl Lewis is a class act. He stands for integrity and honesty and fair play. You are a child of the King. Whatever you do, give it your best and act with integrity. You may not win every time you try but if you lose with dignity, you are still victorious.

"A faith without some doubts is like a human body without antibodies in it. People who blithely go through life too busy or indifferent to ask hard questions about why they believe as they do will find themselves defenseless against either the experience of tragedy or the probing questions of a smart skeptic."

Tim Keller

May 14 2020

Day Fifty-seven

Matthew 6:25-34
"Therefore I tell you, do not be anxious about your life, what you will eat or what you will drink, nor about your body, what you will put on. Is not life more than food, and the body more than clothing? Look at the birds of the air: they neither sow nor reap nor gather into barns, and yet your heavenly Father feeds them. Are you not of more value than they? And which of you by being anxious can add a single hour to his span of life? And why are you anxious about clothing? Consider the lilies of the field, how they grow: they neither toil nor spin, yet I tell you, even Solomon in all his glory was not arrayed like one of these."

Would you consider raising 10,000 children? Maybe not all at once, but over time? The person we speak of today did just that, and he did it all without ever asking for help.

George Mueller lived in Bristol, England in the 1800's. He established 117 Christian schools and he never asked for a dime of help. He trusted in God to give them what they needed for that day, and from reading his writings later, he reported his faith never failed. Even when criticized, even when down to the last bit of flour, at the final moment, just in time, money always came, bread always came, food, clothing always came. Through his schools and churches, he distributed over 285,000 Bibles in twenty languages. Yet, he refused a salary, thinking it would make people feel they had to give, not out of love to God but a sense of duty to George and his wife Mary.

George and Mary used to go for rides and walks around London and he saw the orphans, it seemed like hundreds, begging, stealing, doing whatever they could to survive. It hurt their hearts and tore at their souls. In private they asked God just what He wanted them to do; they couldn't care for them all, and the occasional bread they distributed hardly made a dent in the hunger. After careful planning, George and Mary started their huge work in 1836 when he remodeled his own home to take in 30 little girls, orphans, giving them shelter, food, a home. All he had available was his own home, so he started in his own home.

From that small beginning (if you think caring for 30 girls is a small task!) the need grew. The neighbors complained about the children and the noise so George decided he needed build a separate place in a quieter space; he prayed, land was provided, an architect gave him plans, gifts came in and soon there were girls' and boys' homes, staff members to care for them, and the work grew.

He went one step at a time, raising, teaching, giving the children means to support themselves, and saving thousands. The above verse is said to have been among his favorites. God never let him down. He won't let you down either. Go to Him with your requests, your needs and just in time, he will care for them. He isn't a magic genie; he's a loving Father who has promised to care for us.

Do you want to do great things for God? Start with what you have on hand and give it to Him and it will multiply as you do just what is in front of you.

"God's work done in God's way will never lack God's supplies."
Hudson Taylor

Day Fifty-eight

1 Timothy 4:12

"Let no man despise values, but be an example of the believers, in word, in conversation, in charity, in spirit, in faith, in purity."

In 1964, Italy's Eugenio Monti and Sergio Siopaos were favored to win the two-man bobsled race in the Winter Olympics. Their first run had been wonderful; and as they waited for their second run, they saw that the British team was in a state of despair.

They had had a great first run, but their sled had broken an axle bolt, and they would lose if they couldn't fix it. Monti and Sergio finished their second run and then removed the axle bolt from their bobsled. They gave it to Nash, the British team leader. In one of the greatest upsets in bobsledding, the British team won the gold medal and the sportsmen on the Italian team came in third. Four years later, Monti drove his lead to victory and a gold medal.

Monti knew that lending his bolt could cost him the race. He had seen the first run by the British and knew they were good. But that didn't enter into his deliberations as he spun down the hill on his second run. All he thought of was how terribly disappointing it would be to have to quit for lack of a small part. He was a true sportsman, and didn't hesitate to help his competition. They might have won by withholding the bolt, but to them, helping another athlete to compete was simply the right thing to do.

Have you ever been passed over? You've done your best, you know you'd do well for this or that position but someone else has gone ahead? Have you had the reward for a job you've done go to someone else? Have you given a boost up to someone only to be passed over? Yes, it hurts, but in this life it happens. Take a deep breath, resolve to do your best and go on. You may end up changing jobs completely in order to get ahead; it's inconvenient, it's a little scary, but you go with a good conscience and you start a new place with the knowledge you are doing your best. In the books of Heaven, your efforts will not go unrewarded. It may not make good business sense, but in the currency of heaven, an attitude of helpfulness and forgiveness is legal tender.

Do you know anyone who needs help? Are you willing to do the right thing, even if it might cause you some inconvenience? Christ knew he was going to die when He came to this old earth. He didn't hesitate to come help us. If our Lord can do so much for us, can we bear a little inconvenience and go a little out of our way to help others? Think about it . Remember, we are possibly the only example of Christ some folks will ever meet. Make it count.

"Christian Youth, I need to ask why you sit in the padded pews of your fathers while all around the darkness takes your cities and your friends."
Andrew Strom

Prayer question: Is there someone or some event you need to pray for, to ask wisdom about? Do you need to make a change, or do you need to boost someone else in front of you? Ask for God's guidance in your work life. It changes a job into a witness.

Day Fifty-nine

2nd Timothy 1:7
"For God has not given us the spirit of fear, but of power, and of love, and of a sound mind"

"God saved my life because he knew I could handle it," Chris said. Once you've heard the story, you'll see why this is such an understatement.

Two days before Christmas, Chris and some friends were last-minute shopping and just hanging out. As they drove around, the car hit an icy patch of road and skidded out of control. One kid was thrown from the car and killed instantly. Chris and another boy were catapulted from the car as well. When the ambulance got there, Chris was sitting on the medium. His left leg was lying twenty feet away and blood was gushing out his thigh. He was in a daze of shock and pain. He was rushed to Westbury hospital and into surgery. Seven hours later, as he was waking up, his first question was, "What's going to happen to my basketball career?"

You see, Chris was a great player. As an 8th grader, he had compiled a 41 point average. Now as a freshman, he was playing on the Junior team and in his last 2 games had made 62 points each. He wanted to turn pro someday. His coach came to see him in the hospital and Chris told him he would be back on the team next season. Chris was determined to play again with or without a leg.

Impossible? Only if you don't know the power of prayer and determination. Chris went into therapy to improve his balance and strengthen his body. The pain was unbelievable at times. When he got back home, he worked with a tutor to catch up his school grades. He went to therapy faithfully. And he worked. One day he went outside and looked at the old practice hoop in back of the garage. He put down his crutches and tried to make a basket. Hopping around on one leg, he tried again and again, falling, missing , falling, missing, throwing, falling, missing. After 15 fifteen minutes, he was exhausted, picked up his crutches and went back in the house.

Chris got a prosthesis. He asked how soon he could start playing basketball with it. The doctor knew it usually took a year just to learn to walk on a prosthesis. But he saw the look in Chris's eyes and he felt this boy was going to be different.

Chris spent long hours at home learning to walk, to sit, to just stay in balance. He found it was harder to get baskets with his artificial leg then without. But he kept trying. He got blisters on his stump and wore four socks to cushion it. He hurt more than he thought it was possible to hurt. But he prayed and he worked. He was going to play basketball again this fall in school. His friends came over to visit, and he started to play with his friends outside of school.

Whenever he tried to leave for a rebound, he fell over. When he tried to drive in, he fell down. One day in practicing with the guys, he broke the foot of his prosthesis. It just made him work harder. He began a daily regime of shooting, weightlifting, dribbling. He groaned over his blisters . He tried out for the team that fall. Nobody could believe it, but the coach saw that look in Chris's eyes. He was awkward and clumsy with the ball. But the coach had seen that look in other kids eyes over the years. Chris with was on the team again. Later that week, the coach, announced, "Every year the squad chooses the captain, who is elected because of the example he sets. This year's captain is Chris Samuele." The fellows whooped their joy.

Eight days short of a year since his accident, Chris was playing with his team again. The crowd gave him a standing ovation just for walking out and lining up with the team. He wanted so bad to win, he was so tense he overplayed and couldn't hit the basket. He was taken out of the game for a breather. He talked himself down and the coach put him back in.

He worked himself free about 20 feet from the basket, a teammate passed the ball to him. He launched a high shot and got his first 3 points. The gym crowd went crazy. He did it again and again and again. His team won that night. Chris had made 11 points. He was on his way back.

He continued to play and in several games, he made 30 points. He received letters of interest from colleges and he knew he wanted to coach high school basketball someday. An impossible dream? Only if you don't understand faith and prayer. Chris knew he had a gift from God in his athletic ability and he knew God wanted him to use it. The devil surely tried hard to put a stop to it. He worked and he prayed and he prayed and he worked and he worked some more. And Chris is a champion of the Lord.

"Champions don't give up; they get up!"
Sanjo Jendayi

Day Sixty

Luke 11:13
"If you then, being evil, know how to give good gifts to your children, how much more will your heavenly Father give the Holy Spirit to those who ask Him!"

Scott Wagner was developmentally disabled. That's what the doctors and specialists all said back in 1949 when he was born. "He'll always be a burden to society. Put them away, Mrs. Wagner. That would be best for everyone." Back in the fifties, that what was commonly done with folks that had Down's Syndrome – put them away.

But she didn't do it. She took her boy home with her and trained him to try, to love, and to do his best. Then, when he was 16, his mother died of cancer and his father was unable to care for him, so he ended up at Wood Haven Center; a home for people with developmental handicaps. The experts all said Scott was on the level of a first grader. What the experts couldn't read was his heart, where his genius lay waiting to be discovered.

Scott had been there for 17 years when a man named David, a runner, volunteered to come and teach jogging to the kids at the center. He and Scott started running together.

It wasn't long before they were running miles together. Then they entered their first race together, a 10 km run. That's 6.2 miles. They finished dead last. But it was the first time somebody with Down's syndrome had even entered in endurance race.

Dave and Scott trained more and ran in more races. Each race got longer and harder, but Scott stuck it out. And then came the big one; the Boston marathon. There were 19,000 runners starting. Scott and Dave finished the race in 16,500th place. Is that bad? Could you finish that long a run? I doubt I could walk 26 miles, much less run it. At that time, Scott was the only person with Down's syndrome who had ever even attempted to run a marathon. He was 39. His fans called him, "the King of the Road." At the pinnacle of his career, a silent killer struck the brave young man: he had liver cancer. In a few short months, Scott was dead.

In memory of Scott, the Miami Runner's Club set up a branch called the Achilles Track Club (now Achilles International), which focuses on enabling persons with disabilities to run. His example has inspired other people with handicaps to try hard to be their best. He used his gifts of perseverance and courage to do what no other handicapped person had ever done before. He was a true king in heart.

I've heard some people say they don't feel like they can do anything, that they have no gifts or talents. You have a mind don't you? Scott could only think like a first grader. He had strength of heart, he used his gifts to their fullest extent, and he left a legacy of achievement that anybody could be proud to have.

When you're feeling sorry for yourself, and are being unkind to yourself, stop and think, "I do have gifts. I need to figure them out." Make a list of the gifts you have. If you aren't sure, go online and do a spiritual gifts inventory. Still unsure, ask five people who know you what they think your gifts might be. Put all the research together, see what's in common, and you'll have a pretty good idea where your talents lie. Then brush yourself off, get out there, keep training, and try again.

You may be the only person left who believes in you, but it's enough. It takes just *one star* to pierce a universe of darkness. Never give up.

– Richelle E. Goodrich

Things that Have Shaped Me

In our next few days of worship and learning together, I want to share things that have happened to me personally; things that changed me, molded my character, that made me depend on God. Not so as to boast of anything I have accomplished or done, but in order that I might show you the kind of guidance that God gives; the kind of lessons He uses to teach us, and to bring the glory of those things that have happened to remembrance and to praise He whom we both love. Soli Deo Gloria- the The Glory of God Alone.

May 23 2022

Day Sixty-one

1 Peter 5:7
"Casting all your anxieties on him, because he cares for you."

There is nothing like a house fire to disrupt well laid plans.

Years ago, my husband and I were in the midst of a personal economic downturn. He'd been laid off from work and we'd decided to both go back to school and update our skills. (The company he had worked at for the past nearly fourteen years had been sold and the new company closed down his entire unit. One day he had a performance evaluation that said he was getting a great raise and was doing grand, next day at noon a phone call that he was no longer employed. The next day we left to chaperone at a youth congress and when we got home had to tell the kids what was happening. Talk about an up and down week!)

We had four children at the time. We had sent the kids over to my mom's so I could go out on driving practice. I didn't have a license at the time, and after the first few months of unemployment, we knew I needed to go out and help earn money so I got a permit to learn and we went out to practice almost daily. We'd been out on a driving practice run when we returned, saw smoke, opened the front door and immediately tossed our two little Pomeranian dogs into the yard. I ran to my folks' place two doors down to call the firemen. I found the kids were all safe there, watching TV. I told them to stay put, and I ran back to wait with Dan .We helplessly stood watching while they broke windows, stormed the house, spraying water, getting it all out. We were told that our daughter's precious saltwater fish tank in the basement rec room was all that saved us from losing our home completely: it blew up in the heat, spilling fifty five gallons of water on the flames, turning them to steam. Some rodent had gnawed at electric wiring and now our home was a sodden, covered in soot and smoke mess. Opening the windows wide, propping open doors to let the smoke out, we stayed at my mom's that night, camping on the floor. After him losing his job we didn't think we could feel any lower.

What had disturbed me the most was this was Wednesday night; in our church that meant prayer meeting. As we helplessly watched the firemen fighting the fire, breaking windows, chopping through the roof, standing there in the twilight holding our little dogs, people we knew lined their cars up across the street to watch the fire on their way to church. Not one got out and came over to see if they could help.. I heard later they announced it at prayer meeting and they all prayed for us. In the ensuing days, however, not one contacted us with an offer of help

But the college that we attended was a Christian college; the President called with offers of help; students came over to help clean. We found out that God is faithful. I hauled all the smoky linens to the local laundromat and they gave me a discount on washing and drying them. We were blessed with gift cards to local fast food places so we could eat until I was able to get the kitchen clean once more and in commission. A garbage company loaned us the use of a dumpster for a couple days so we could unload all the damaged stuff; the Red Cross had contacted them.

I passed my driver's test two weeks later and found work the same week. When a bill came, we always seemed to have just enough to pay it. We always had food and though the basement was pretty much gutted out, there was no bad structural damage. We lost most of our library to water and smoke, but the important books, the kid's study books (they were homeschooled) were not touched. The laundry waiting in the basement to be washed was destroyed, but the local thrift store run by Interchurch gave me a voucher to come and get clothes for each of us for free; actually better than what we had, which had been pretty well worn out. Within three months, the house was clean, we were back in classes, I had work that would bring income we needed, and I learned that when others fail you, God has a way. He never fails us.

"When all you have is God, you have all you need."
Dennis Fisher

Day Sixty-two

Philippians 4:6-7

"Do not be anxious about anything, but in everything by prayer and supplication with thanksgiving let your requests be made known to God. And the peace of God, which surpasses all understanding, will guard your hearts and your minds in Christ Jesus."

To me this has been the hardest verse in the Bible to take to heart. I am a natural worrier. I don't do so badly at praising God when something is going well; it's when everything is seemingly going south for no apparent reason I have difficulty staying optimistic. When it seems we have spiritual saber tooth tigers eating our confidence, I turn into a worrier as my normal default setting. I have had to learn worrying simply short circuits our peace with nothing to show for it.

Many years ago, I was an expectant mom; this was going to be my third child, I thought I had it all figured out. I couldn't wait to hold my baby; this one, I had been told, was a boy. I had two darling girls but a son was just going to be grand. I was so impatient for him to show his face to the world and to me.

When the labor pains came, I waited to be sure they weren't Braxton-hicks (a false alarm.) I told Danny and he, as always, broke land speed records getting me to the hospital which was really only two miles away. We had plenty of time, but well, Dan worries too.

I got checked in and then labor stopped. However, rather than go home, the doctor decided there was fetal distress and I ended up having a C-section. Trouble was, little Miah wasn't ready and when I came out of the anesthesia, it was to have a nurse asking my permission to rush him to Columbus Children's Hospital or he might not make it. They brought him in for me to see; his head was in a green plastic box, receiving enriched oxygen because he couldn't breathe. He was premature. He could die by morning or before without the right care and even perhaps with it. I signed in a blur. I couldn't read the paper because no one handed me my glasses. They asked if I wanted to see his face but when they lifted the cover so I could, the baby gasped and shook. I told them to cover him with the face mask again and please take good care of my boy. And he was gone.

I had nightmares that night of him gasping for air like he was drowning. He was so little. His sisters had been eight pounders; he came in at under five. Describing how it felt the next morning when I could hear the nurses rolling the other mother's babies to them in little plastic basket beds, everyone else had their babies brought to them for nursing and I hadn't even been able to hold my child is almost impossible. The reports I was getting from the hospital sixty miles away weren't good. Miah wasn't getting stronger, he was losing ground. Despair, dismay, self-recriminations all ran through my head. I demanded to know why God let this happen. And in that quiet way of His, as I lie on the bed sniffling, in pain from surgery, (it hurts to sob after abdominal surgery), as I calmed down, the realization came to me that God was here with me, even here. He was with Miah and He gives good gifts to his children. And who was I to presume to tell the Creator of all that is how to run the Kingdom? I gave my son to God then. Even if I might not be able to hold him before he might pass away, still, the Lord giveth, the Lord taketh away, blessed be the name of the Lord. A warm feeling of peace came over me. I started to nap but God had a different plan.. My nap was interrupted by yet another nurse checking on me.

  This OB nurse suggested I pump milk and send it to the baby. She asked if I had anyone who could take it to him so he would bond to me when he got better. She brought a variety of pumps, we experimented and at least my breasts weren't aching anymore. I gave the sterile tube of milk to Danny and he began the first of twice daily milk runs to Columbus. He said Little Miah was in iffy shape until he started getting milk from me. Then he started to gain some strength. His weight and breathing chart had rapidly been going rapidly down, but when he got my milk, he shot up suddenly.

  Back then, you stayed in the hospital for seven days for a caesarian. (We didn't have the lower bikini incisions then, they cut you from just below your navel to your lower abdomen-I still have a seven inch scar.) On the fifth day, the Doctor allowed me to go home, but only to rest. He ordered me not to try and drive to Columbus. The OB ward was busy, they were sending home folks who normally wouldn't be sent home because they needed the rooms. I got in the car and told Dan to head for Columbus. I leaned back and napped. (I never have been good at following orders…) Compared to my other two babies, Miah was so small, so weak and so beautiful. All the pain of the last week went away and I held my baby. He was our newest special gift from God,. Now he's over six feet tall, has sons of his own, works hard to provide for his family. He has always been a special son.

"He who lays up treasures on earth spends his life backing away from his treasures. To him, death is loss. He who lays up treasures in heaven looks forward to eternity; he's moving daily toward his treasures. To him, death is gain."

Randy Alcorn

Day Sixty-three

Isaiah 41:10

"Fear not, for I am with you; be not dismayed, for I am your God; I will strengthen you, I will help you, I will uphold you with my righteous right hand."

Years ago, life got to be too much for me. I was a young mother, at home with three children, a fourth on the way, and a husband who traveled in his work. I lived in a half finished house where the roof sometimes leaked, where the wood fire had to be constantly managed or it would be too cold, with a church congregation and pastor who felt since I was a stay at home mom, I ought to have more church offices since I "obviously had time and ability" to do them all. I had no way to get out as I didn't drive and frankly, although I had a wagon I could put all three kids in and drag it on errands, it was exhausting. Being pregnant didn't help.

In addition, we were homeschoolers. I had a big garden in the summer. And slowly, the stress and the strain and the work got me, and my health crashed. I had severe panic attacks. I was in the hospital six times, a few days each time, over a period of three months. I ended up with a Holter monitor and a heart catheterization and echocardiogram and a bunch of tests I don't recall. Life was too scary. I quit going anywhere unless my husband or another adult was there. I was done with adulting. I was so frightened by my life, by my own mind and the paranoid ideations I thought up I was afraid to stay at home alone, so on nights when Dan was off working my mom would come over and sleep at our place. I quit going to church, I stopped singing. I felt totally, absolutely lost.

And worst, I couldn't read my Bible. When I would start, I'd go into a panic attack and all I could find there seemed against me. Until you've been on the bad side of depression and ill health, you don't know how many verses are in there that can be misconstrued as God being mad at you!

It wasn't until a Christian counselor gave me a list of texts like the one above I started to feel I could crawl out of the hole I was in. It was the first text on the list; I memorized it, I sang it to myself when the waves of fear would attack, I wrote it over and over. And that's what made it all break: I started to write about what I felt, what I knew was truth, and started to look outside my own problems. I started doing just what I could. I visited old people; they seemed harmless and when I and the kids would show up with a copy of that week's sermon and some homemade cookies, the welcome we got soothed me and made me feel I was still a capable person.

I got out in the garden again and planted more flowers. I gradually reentered life. Now, whenever I start feeling that temptation to just give it up I remember this verse. I sing it in my head. I hear it in my soul. The panic dies and I am comforted. I recall my blessings; I recall His love and the love of family and I know this path is the one He chose for me to learn from and to get me to slow down and consider more important things.

"God never said that the journey would be easy, but He did say that the arrival would be worthwhile"
Max Lucado

Day Sixty-four

Isaiah 46:4

"I am your God and will take care of you until you are old and your hair is gray. I made you and will care for you; I will give you help and rescue you."

As I get older, (and the line to what is older keeps flexing in my mind), I find that getting old is not for wimps. There are aches and pains and stumbles I never had when I was young. There is comfort in knowing that He is watching over me. Sometimes I really need it. Go back with me in my memory to when my oldest child was in college and we were headed to visit and celebrate Valentine's day…

My husband and I, our two teen sons and two infant grandchildren were heading up to Michigan to visit Fawn who was in graduate school. I took first driving on the trip since we would be driving for six hours to get there. I drive better in daylight and since we hadn't been able to leave until after we both got home from work, I was at the wheel. The night came up fast and it was snowing and blowing. I didn't realize how bad the road was as I mentally ticked off the things in my head, being sure I'd not forgotten something. Like any mom, you know, diapers, check, kids, check, read books so the boys wouldn't be bored, check, Bible, checks, clothes, check, surprise sheet cake for the dorm party,...you know how mom's obsess sometimes.

We came to the interstate and I turned on, headed on 23 to our next turn-off. I was looking for a place to pull over so Dan could drive and knew there was a rest area not far ahead. All seemed fine, kids were asleep, Dan and I were discussing how bad the roads were, how the surprise Valentine's day cake we were bringing Fawn would be a hit in the dorm when suddenly, just as I came to an overpass, the van hit black ice.

We skidded, I did everything they told me to do in the required by my work safe driving school: turned into the slide, foot off gas, let the car slow, no brakes. We banged onto the concrete barrier and bounced back a little as we came to rest. The kids were shaken awake and crying: I explained that we'd banged into a bridge, everything was fine, settle down. Dan got out to assess the damage.

The rest of traffic just whizzed past us by as if the road was fine, no black ice or snow. I heard Dan say, "Got to get tool out of the back to pull the bumper from the wheel. Other than that, I think she's drivable," was his verdict. "Everybody, just stay put for a couple minutes. We'll pull into the rest area and check diapers and such. Wife, move over to the other side. I'm driving from here."

I got out, moved to the passenger seat, got in, shut the door and bent down to get bottles for the babies. I heard Dan scream "Watch out!" And the van seemed to take on a life of its own. God help us! I cried just before hitting my head on the dash. The world spun and rocked and it felt as if we were going to flip. We settled back and wobbled and cold wind blew in from the back where Dan had been standing, getting tools. Where was my husband?

    "A God wise enough to create me and the world I live in is wise enough to watch out for me."
                                        Philip Yancey

Day Sixty-five

Deuteronomy 31:6
"Be strong and courageous. Do not be afraid or terrified because of them, for the Lord your God goes with you; he will never leave you nor forsake you."

I felt the car tilt over the bridge barrier and suddenly right itself, as if pushed back, wobbled a little, and stop still. The kids kept screaming. I felt the bump on my head, a real knot was forming. I called back to the boys. "Are you ok?"

Ben yelled back, "Mom, the car may blow up, we've got to get out of it." In my head I thought, way too many cop shows and then realized he was right.

Taking a deep breath, I agreed and we all got out into the February winter night; it was snowing harder. Later I found the wind chill had been below zero. Miah had blood running down his face from a cut, Ben unclipped and handed out the car seats to me. I covered the babies with their blankets. Little Tristain was strangely silent but Alana was screaming. We looked for Dan. Ben saw him first. Dan was lying underneath the steel bridge rails, and he wasn't moving. There was blood dripping from the rail onto his chest. Ben gasped, "Mom, you got to save dad. He can't die. You have to save dad."

I told them to huddle together, grab their coats from the car. I got my cape out of the front seat and an old pink comforter we kept in the van for emergencies. I put my shoulder purse over my shoulder and dashed over to Dam. He was barely conscious.

"Dan, keep talking to me. Don't go to sleep," I said as I covered him with the comforter. I finally started praying. Looking up, I saw the boys talking to a stranger. He came over.

"Ma'am, we won't let nothing through except ambulances and cops," he started to say. I looked up and saw semi-trucks parked across the road in all six lanes; all their emergency lighting on, men running around placing flares. "Ambulances will be here shortly but those babies are going to freeze. I'm going to take your boys and the babies to my truck cab: it's that big blue one right there. You can see them from here. They can stay there while I put out flares and the police come. Don't you worry none. The cops will be here soon. We've called them and God's got this under control, lady. I'll be right back."

I saw the man who had hit us. He had been driving a red sports car faster than he ought to and hit the black ice, then spun and hit us. He stumbled into the side of the car getting out. His girlfriend got out and was leaning against the car, throwing up. I kept talking to Dan. It was terribly cold and he and I were shivering, our teeth chattering. I tucked the comforter up and tucked his sweater from the car under his head to get his head out of the snow. I kept praying. Truckers came over, they were putting flares everywhere. Two truckers came over and started to pray quietly behind me as I held Dan's hand. The first one came over and said he had his heater turned up full and the kids were warming up.

"I thought that van was going to go over that bridge, I really did," said one. "It was tilted way over."

"I's God's grace, that's what it was. That van was pushed back where it belonged, no other excuse for it," opined another. I heard sirens in the distance. I looked up and saw a truck move forward and police and ambulances start pouring through the hole, and the truck backed up to block it again. I heard horns blowing in the distance. It started snowing again and the wind picked up. All I could do was hold Dan's hand and pray we would all make it.

"The greater your knowledge of the goodness and grace of God on your life, the more likely you are to praise Him in the storm."

Matt Chandler

May 28 2020

Day Sixty-six

Psalm 118:6
"The Lord is with me; I will not be afraid. What can mere mortals do to me?"

A policeman came over to where I was, along with EMT's who had a stretcher. I watched as they loaded the stretcher with my broken husband and nearly ran it to the ambulance.

"Lady, are you all right?" The state trooper looked impossibly young to me. He was so tall I had to look up and squint at him through the wind and snow.

"I don't know. My husband is hurt bad. I don't know where my children are? And I'm dizzy."

"Ambulance just got here and they've got all four of your kids in it and are heading to have them checked out at the hospital. They're leaving in that one that just pulled out. Come over here out of the wind, ma'am."

"They'll need our insurance cards. Dan's wallet is in the car he never drives with it in his pocket."

"Let me see if I can get that for you." He looked in the front, got the wallet, and the registration from our van, and came back. He wrote things on his report and an EMT came over.

"We need to get you all to the hospital, lady. You have to be checked out." The policeman put the papers in the wallet and handed it to me. I stuffed it in my purse.

I turned and looked and I tried not to notice the blood on the rail so much. I started to crumple and the EMT caught me. I sat down on the stretcher and they strapped me in place. I heard a siren start up; I felt us move.

There were two of us in the ambulance and there was a strong order of alcohol. I looked over and saw the man who had hit us was in the ambulance as well, strapped down so he'd not fall off the stretcher.
The EMT did a fast check of vitals and suddenly began cutting my clothing down the front.

"What are you doing?" I asked.

"You're suffering from shock and cold and you'll get warmer without being covered up," he said

"I need a blanket," I insisted. "I can't just lie here hanging out like this." He was busy putting electrodes on my chest and neck. He started an IV.

The man in the other stretcher keep looking me up and down as I lie there naked and all I could think of was this dress had been made for me by my daughter who I was going up to visit. She'd given it to me on my last birthday and I wanted to show her how well it fit. Now it was cut in two. I'd never mend it well enough to hide that. For some irrational reason I kept trying to figure out ways to sew it together and cover the cutting with lace. I looked over and the guy who may have killed my husband was leering at me, less than three feet away and I was strapped down helpless to even cover myself. He reached over to try and poke me and the EMT pushed his hand back.

"I must insist I be covered," I tried to sound firm. "This is beyond immodest." My teeth were chattering and I was so cold, so very cold.

"No, you'll get warm faster if you're uncovered," replied the EMT. "We're nearly to the hospital. Hold on just a few more minutes." The man beside me belched loudly and reached for me again. I could not evade him, as even my arms were strapped down. He had somehow gotten his arm out. and the EMT was busy with machinery.

By now I was getting agitated. I was strapped onto the stretcher, I could not get away. "Lord, Be with my kids and my husband and get us together again soon. And please, keep protecting us." I tried to turn my head to not look at the other passenger. My head was strapped in place. I closed my eyes. That got the EMT's attention.

"Lady, keep your eyes open. Do not fall asleep on me!" I opened them, fixed them on a spot on the ceiling and continued to pray. The man next to me started to snore suddenly and the EMT leaned over to check him, shaking his head., "He's sleeping off his drunk, but he's still alive. Can't get him awake from that." The man's arm hung down over the side of the stretcher. The EMT kept putting it back up on his chest, but for some reason, he wasn't strapped down as I was. We rolled on through the night, lights flashing through the windows, siren blaring.

"God's angels often protect his servants from potential enemies."
Billy Graham

May 29th 2020

Day Sixty-seven

Romans 8:28 "And we know that for those who love God all things work together for good, for those who are called according to his purpose."

When we arrived at the hospital, a blanket was finally put over me and they swooshed me in through the doors and into a waiting room. The usual blood tests were taken. I could hear my babies crying in the hall. I asked the nurse how my husband was, where were the kids, what was going on.

They told me Dan was in emergency surgery, she'd check on the kids. I waited. Finally I started to yell, since the call button didn't work. A nurse came in and I demanded to know what was happening. She told me she didn't know and left. I was still strapped down (I was told this was so I wouldn't hurt my neck if it were broken.)

The hospital social worker came in to give me paperwork to sign. She said I was going in for an x-ray and they could unstrap me then. I asked about the kids. I couldn't hear them anymore. She smiled. "The babies are fine. They had x-rays and now they're running all over the

ER. We're going to corral them in a room with an aide watching them until your family gets here to take them. Your boys had some stitches but they're ok as well. The boys told us how to contact your family and they're all going to go home with your folks who are coming up to get them. It's going to take them awhile to get here because the roads are bad. Your dad said to tell you Tiny was driving since he has more experience with cold weather driving. I know I'm not supposed to say anything because no one signed releases, but I think if you stop worrying a bit, you'll do better. After the x-ray, the doctor will be in to update you." I thanked her.

I had the x-ray and nothing was broken but they couldn't stop my heart from jumping around, or my blood pressure from dancing the tarantella. I asked about my husband and was told he'd be out of surgery soon. The next doctor spoke to me and ordered I be given updates on Dan and that I would be admitted because they were concerned about my heart. I explained I had PAT disease (paroxysmal atrial tachycardia and told them what my medications were, they were in my purse. They took the medications and I asked them to contact my doctor back home. And then the parade started.

The first nurse told me that Danny had to have a tube put in for a collapsed lung and now he could breathe. They were trying to clean out his scalp so they could stitch his head.

The next one came in and told me he'd had a greenfield filter put in his groin so clots wouldn't kill him.

The next told me he had a severe concussion.

The next said he'd had internal bleeding but they were pretty sure they had it stopped.

The next told me he'd never walk normally again because all the ligaments in his knee had been severed and his leg was basically being held on by his thick skin. Everything else was a mash and they might have to amputate.

The next told me his arm was broken and was being set with steel plates to hold it in place. They couldn't guarantee his hand would not be affected and more than likely he'd never play piano again.

Yet another came in and said his spleen and pancreas had been injured badly. The first one came back to tell me they'd gotten the excess liquid out of his lungs, but were keeping the chest tube.

Another came in and told me again they were keeping me because my heart was beating irregularly. (You think?)

Still, before Dan was taken up to ICU, where I was going as well, they let me see him. I was in a wheelchair, he was on a stretcher, still woozy. He groggily smiled at me; I patted his hand and held it as we had prayer together. I gave him what I knew about the kids.

"Guess I get to stay awhile, dear," he said. "Be sure to call my boss and let him know." I didn't tell him I was being admitted too and wouldn't be calling anytime soon.

"God does not remove us from all harm; He uses harm to move us close to Him."

Dillon Burrough

May 30 2000

Day Sixty-eight

Psalm 91:1-16

"He who dwells in the shelter of the Most High will abide in the shadow of the Almighty. I will say to the LORD, "My refuge and my fortress, my God, in whom I trust." For he will deliver you from the snare of the fowler and from the deadly pestilence. He will cover you with his pinions, and under his wings you will find refuge; his faithfulness is a shield and buckler. You will not fear the terror of the night, nor the arrow that flies by day ..."

My dad and brother arrived and I saw them briefly and told them what happened. They took the kids home to stay a few days until I could get home.

I filled out more paperwork and explained to the staff in the step down unit that I had PAT disease (paroxysmal Atrial Tachycardia.) and the medications I was on; however, the hospital couldn't get into my doctor until Monday, this was Friday so they could not verify the diagnosis and they started giving me whatever med they thought might help. Somehow the medications I'd given the ER doctor had not gone upstairs with me. I learned much about medications over the next few hours.

Nitro glycerin makes the top of your head feel like it's blowing off and leaves you with an awful migraine if you don't have the disease it's made for. I don't.

The yellow pill makes you see double. It increases heart rate which I didn't need. They brought in a defibrillator just in case I went into that state while waiting for the opposite drug they then gave me had time to work and slow my heartbeat down.

The small capsule makes you barf. I was really sick of nausea by the end of that one.

The green pill makes your BP plummet and makes you faint, making them give you another pill to bring it back up, and that pill makes your heart beat fast again.

The next pill, a pink one as I recall, makes you very woozy and somewhat slap happy and unfocused, and when that one hit, I refused to take anymore and they thought I was unreasonable…

And for some odd reason only known to my subconscious, the rock song kept going through my head, interrupting my mental prayers…

"One pill makes you bigger
And one pill makes you small
And the ones that Mother gives you
Don't do anything at all…"(Jefferson Airplane, White Rabbit)

Next morning they got through to my doctor's office and were set straight on what my medications were (oddly enough, exactly what I had in my purse when all this started)and I was given the correct things and everything calmed down. Other than cracked ribs, a concussion, several stitches, for glass cuts, and really bad whiplash, I was fine and was released Tuesday to go home. Dan was transferred to Grant Trauma center in Columbus, Ohio. He had three more surgeries to go but was stable. I didn't get to see him again for a week. I had nothing to drive frankly, I didn't think I ever wanted to drive again. I got in touch with Dan's company and told them what happened. I got in touch with my agency and told them what happened.

And God was still protecting us and still providing for us.

"My focus is not on the flood that surrounds me. Rather, my focus is on the God Who surrounds the flood."
                                        Craig D. Lounsbrough

May 31 2020

Day Sixty-nine

Isaiah 54:17
"No weapon that is fashioned against you shall succeed, and you shall confute every tongue that rises against you in judgment. This is the heritage of the servants of the LORD and their vindication from me, declares the LORD."

I went home, called all the various jobs, told them what happened. I drove my husband's little fiesta for a few days after I returned to work, but it would hardly hold me, let alone my kids or my clients. I had to have a vehicle yet we didn't have the funds. I'd paid out to Doctors and pharmacies and regular bills what we had saved up. I had to locate a car, and I told God I knew there would be lots of bills from this and we simply couldn't have a car payment. I had to have a large vehicle that seats at least 7 and had room for groceries and I had to have cash for it.

I talked to my insurance company and to the lawyer we had engaged. (It appears the man who hit us was drunk, he was with a lady other than his wife and he was going to sue us for having been stopped on the bridge, so we got a lawyer at the suggestion of our insurance man.) The lawyer and the insurance got together and provided me $10,000 to get a safe vehicle, based on the fact that my van was pretty well totaled and this was what it had been worth before.

I took the check to my bank and deposited it, then in the bank parking lot, I bent my head and asked God to help me. I knew nothing about picking a car. Dan always did that stuff. I wouldn't know a good one from a bad one. I couldn't make a mistake in choosing a vehicle. Dan was still in the hospital. I'd get no second chance to get this right.

On my first visit to the car lot, I saw a vehicle, test drove it and felt safe in it. It was, quite simply, a very large vehicle. I ended up buying a 1990 Suburban. Lovingly called the Subdivision by the kids, it was a great vehicle that made you feel brave to drive. You sat way up high in it; you could see all around; it had big windows and lots of space. I drove it for some years.

In the meantime, Dan was still in Columbus having surgeries; the kids had come home when I did, but we didn't feel whole without Dan. I prayed God would put our family back together. Ben and Miah were having flashbacks. God provided a counselor that helped them quickly regain their emotional strength.

Dan was still in the hospital and came home in about a month. They had rebuilt his knee. He had a full length cast on his leg and was on crutches. When the casts came off his arm and his leg, he went to physical therapy and was told if they could get him walking again, it was going to take a lot of work. He would always have a bad limp, if he walked at all. He might be able to get his leg to bend at a 90 degree angle. He might never play organ again if they couldn't get his arm to settle down and heal properly. So we prayed.

Dan not only walks today, he runs. He works on our farm making hay, caring for animals. He plays the organ for church. He tells us that when he saw the car careening out of control, coming for us, he yelled watch out! Then he cried God save us.

We went back and looked at the van and figured out where the other car hit. The physics of the accident were all wrong. Witnesses said they saw the van tip over and it should have gone over the bridge and plunged to the interstate underneath, but halfway over, it looked like it had been pushed up against gravity. Dan says he should have been squished like a bug, he was right between the car hurtling for him and the van and no way to get out of the way due to the van doors blocking him on either side but he felt someone push him up in the air and toss him aside; he remembers flying and hitting the rail and he remembers watching as he the van swerved and tipped as it was hit by the sports car. To this day, he calls it being pushed by an angel. I think he was right about that. It could have been so much worse.

And you know the very oddest thing about it all? The next story is about poverty and how it can happen to anyone; and how God can reimburse us for the years the locusts have taken. I know it sounds like I'm babbling, but read on to what was the lead up to this accident. It's a very strange way to have a prayer answered. It will fit together as a whole after the next few studies.

"The violent winds of suffering and trouble blow us into the Lord's protective hands."

Sadhu Sundar Singh

June 1 2020

Day Seventy

Habakkuk 3:17-19

"Though the fig tree should not blossom, nor fruit be on the vines, the produce of the olive fail and the fields yield no food, the flock be cut off from the fold and there be no herd in the stalls, yet I will rejoice in the Lord; I will take joy in the God of my salvation. God, the Lord, is my strength; he makes my feet like the deer's; he makes me tread on my high places."

Remember I mentioned the year Dan had been laid off, when we had the house fire? In the timeline of our marriage, this story is between that story and the accident. The two little ones had not been born yet; Beni was the youngest in the family.

I remember when we told the kids that their dad had lost his job. There was a long silence, then Beni, age 8, said, "Does this mean we'll never have peanut butter again?" It broke the shock, we assured him God would always provide food for us. I was so thankful we had no mortgage. We knew this was going to be hard; we just had no idea how tough. We had a savings, we figured we could live frugally on that and Dan would find a new job.

We prayed and asked God for help, and tended our garden. Now in the unreal fairy tale world that we sometimes hear in churches, we'd all live on an abundant garden and be happy but the reality was the garden failed that year.

We'd grown good gardens every other year but this year, what the squash beetles didn't eat, the potato beetles and tomato hornworms and other bugs did. We watered from our artesian well but it was as if the heat just wouldn't stop. We ran out of food in the house. We had nothing in the garden but some tomatoes, corn and a couple cucumbers. My kids were hungry. Dan put out over three hundred applications and got nary a nibble. His unemployment was running out.

I was raised in a hardworking, middle class family; I'd taken pride in my family and my home. We had never been wealthy but we always had enough for me to be a stay at home mom. Dan's unemployment ran out, he worked at various odd jobs but there simply wasn't enough to pay the utilities and buy food. He started a part time business, he mowed lawns, he repaired things, I babysat for friends. It wasn't enough. There came a day when for the last three days, all we'd had to eat were corn, tomatoes and scrambled eggs from my dad's hens. We didn't even have enough flour to make some biscuits. My kids were hungry. After discussion, prayer and advice from my parents, I swallowed and went to apply for welfare, something I had never thought I'd have to do.

I found out what so many poor folks had found before me; applying for welfare is hard work. There is an initial appointment; then you fill out reams of paper, and collect everyone's birth certificates and social security cards, and last pay stubs and proof of who lives there…and turn it all in to be scrutinized.

And then you find out when you get the medical insurance cards that your family doctor doesn't like taking them; you find when you go shopping you don't go to this store you always did because people say cutting things to you as you check out that you never thought you'd hear; things like "why don't you just go get a job?"
" Welfare mom, bet you've never paid taxes in your life."
" You people have nothing to do but stay home and have kids taxpayers have to support."
And that was just the checkout clerks in the store I'd been buying my groceries at for the past ten years.

You go to another store where they're used to dealing with people "like you." Since you've been a stay at home mom, you're ordered to do WEP hours to "get you used to the workforce." Dan was required to go; he'd had a job, he was actively looking and turning in his contacts to them; they considered him already rehabilitated but I was a stay at home mom. That could not be allowed.

I could not help thinking, sometimes bitterly, that for six years before marriage, I paid taxes, and Dan had paid them since he started working at age 14. Between us, twenty years of taxes had been paid in. Now that we needed, as it were, some of them back to survive, we were treated like mongrel dogs.

You're required to sit through movies of people trying to tell you to just go look for a job with benefits and you feel so ashamed and so much like a failure and you really haven't done anything. They actually give you a reading test to see if you can read well enough to fill out a job application. They require you to get a physical to be sure you're healthy enough to work. And then they assign you to work at a local charity until you find work. I didn't mind that so much. I'd done volunteer work for years.

However, volunteering and WEP hours were different. I had to carry full sacks of groceries being given to people up two flights of stairs all afternoon; the food in this food bank was in the basement. Another person filled the bags, I carried them upstairs for six hour shifts. I pulled my back out. My doctor said not to do it. I took a note from him to the director, and she told me I could not be excused from it, take aspirin and get the bags up, maybe only carry one at a time, not two, which meant twice as many trips. I could not call off or our food stamps would be cut. I had no idea why we were being tested this way. We had always been tithe paying, faithful to our duty and this could not be happening. Dan could do nothing to help.

"When you understand that life is a test, you realize that nothing is insignificant in your life "
Rick Warren

Day Seventy-one

Psalm 32:5
"Then I acknowledged my sin to you and did not cover up my iniquity. I said, "I will confess my transgressions to the LORD." And you forgave the guilt of my sin."

I continued to work twenty-five hours a week at the food pantry; Dan continued to look for work; nothing showed up for us. He still worked at several odd jobs and being honest folks, he reported them.

You would have thought he'd dropped a bomb in the lobby. They demanded receipts, which, since he is methodical, he actually had. They informed him he was supposed to be actively looking for work, not trying to start an underground business. (He mowed eight lawns weekly as I recall, earning about ninety dollars a week.) They immediately cut our food stamps. They accused us of fraud even though we had followed directions and reported the income. And they increased my WEP hours to "pay back what we had not reported before." (Actually, we had reported it and it had been dismissed as fine before. We had a new caseworker now. It appears she felt it was wrong.)

So while we are waiting out in the lobby to discover if there are going to be charges brought against us, I picked up a flyer about a new program where you went back to school, earned a degree and it counted as your WEP hours and enabled you to be retrained for honest work. (Entrepreneurship being obviously not honest, nor as I think back, was motherhood.)

I asked about it and discovered suddenly that I was what was called a displaced homemaker. I could indeed sign up for classes as long as I started within the next three weeks of the program deadline. At one of the agencies I was doing WEP hours in, I met a social worker. She encouraged me to go back to school. She saw something in me I didn't at that point see in myself. I wasn't "just a housewife." She gave me the courage to go back to college at 41. I thought I was too old to learn.

Dan and I discussed it; there was a Christian college on the list of accepted campuses, and we both applied. I made phone calls to different major professors and the programs kept being filled because, after all, it was end of July, classes started in three weeks and there was simply no way to be accepted in time. I was refused to even apply in nursing, education, medical assisting, even just getting in pre-requisites. I was desperate, I was scared and I was depressed. My panic attacks returned.

I started thinking of the lady who had encouraged me and although I knew nothing of what it took, I decided to try one more program. That's when I met the head of the Social Work department, Karen Boyd. Karen is very kind person who explained what the field actually was about and it sounded like something I could do. She told me where to hand walk my admission forms, how to speed up the process and she'd be more than glad to have me enter her major. She made calls for me to get referrals. She encouraged me and lo and behold, I was in line at registration.

I was scared so bad the first few days. I worried I wouldn't be able to keep up with the youngsters in my classes. It had been over twenty years since I'd sat in a college class. Within a short time, I realized they were having trouble keeping up with me…and I spent the next 25 years of my life helping others, mostly the poor and desperate and hurting to find peace. Would I have done this if I stayed at home raising my own? I doubt it. He had to shove me out of my comfortable place, so I could run on high places with Him.

Dan was accepted into the ministry program. He had a marvelous time working with the Nazarene faculty, arguing points of doctrine; he is a rabbi at heart and he was in his element. My WEP hours stopped. My back quit aching. Dan's frantic looking for work slowed. True, we had this form we had to fill out each week; for every class, after class, we had to have our professor sign it to prove we had not missed class. We were not allowed to miss a single class or our benefits would be impacted. It was embarrassing to be known as those old people who were here on welfare. We accumulated student loans (the program did not have grants attached; if we went to school, we had to pay for it. You were just given food stamps and a medical card sand expected to live off the money left over from the costs of classes; in short, to build up debt to survive. It was supposed to get you out of the welfare system.)

We kept this up for almost two years; Dan found work full time after the first year and dropped out of the program. He later completed it in another way but that's a story for later. I found work as a nurse's aide but still continued with school and graduated. It had been a hard three and a half years since he had lost his first position. We were eighteen thousand dollars in debt, (we'd had none before) but we were employed, we had weathered this storm and we hoped life would settle down.

At the time, it appeared God had not heard our pleas for help. I know now that all these things happened so that later, I would know what being poor felt like and be able to leave my middle class mindset and actually care about the people I would meet later. And God is faithful. After our horrible accident, the funds from the accident's aftermath paid off the student loans and other bills that had accumulated. God got us trained for our life work, and He saw the bills were paid; it wasn't easy, but looking back, I see why it all happened the way it did.

God does not give us everything we want, but He does fulfill His promises, leading us along the best and straightest paths to Himself."
     Dietrich Bonhoeffer

Day Seventy-two

Psalm 46:1
God is our refuge and strength, a very present help in times of trouble.

I am a cancer survivor; I have been in remission for twelve years. I can remember like it was yesterday the doctor telling me, on waking up from a biopsy, that he had good news and bad news. The bad was I had Hodgkin's lymphoma and the good was that with aggressive treatment I had at least a 35% chance of making it. I had four kids at home, two others were adults by now, a good job I loved, a husband I adored and a 55% chance of being dead in six months…

People ask me what went through my mind on being told I had to take an indefinite leave of absence, get my affairs in order, just in case, be in the hospital for a port to be installed in four days, and start treatment immediately. Your entire world is thrown into chaos.

I showed up at work the same day to clean out my desk, fill in all that paperwork (family medical leave act, and applying for extended leave, papers saying as far as I knew this was not a workman's' comp case? Really?) and prepare my friends and family to enter the fight of my life. I called the family together to meet in two days and we had a discussion on what was going on so everyone was on the same page. I sent letters to all my clients explaining I would be on extended leave and others would be taking over for me. My supervisor assigned all my cases to others. There was no time for closure for any of them; there was no time for closure for me. I didn't know if I'd be back. Dan came in and we loaded everything into boxes and took the boxes down to my truck the next morning before anyone got there. I got it all out, packed in boxes and put away in my storage closet with a vow I would someday reverse the process and carry it all back.

    I was told my long hair would fall out, all of it, so it would be best for my plumbing at home if I just cut it short now. I had never cut my hair. It was black, hung below my waist, and was my one vanity. I went down and got it cut the next day at a lovely shop where the owner was very kind: she told me all about an organization that donated wigs to chemo ladies. I didn't want a wig. I wanted my hair. I took it home and stored it in my cedar chest.

    My secretary was in tears at work when she saw my hair cut like a boy; when I had Danny come in and haul out my things from the office, when they held a surprise 'good by for now, get well' party for me I had to fight back the tears as well. I still have the teddy bear they gave me. Their emails helped me over the hard times.

    And then I went to the hospital to start the long process.

The verse above was my rock. I kept saying it like a mantra over the next ten months of treatment. When they had to do an MRI, I sang it to myself. I've always been a little claustrophobic. It seems to take forever that you are inside listening to the clanging of the machine. You are held in tight by straps, your head in a cage so you don't move anything and then the table goes in and out, clang, clang, clang. They play music-in this case they gave me a choice of a local radio station or a tape they had there. Not knowing, I just said play whatever and I spent the next hour in the machine listening to some pretty obnoxious reggae. (Somehow the don't worry be happy mindset doesn't fit in an MRI machine. The happy beat doesn't match the clanging and can be quite disorienting..) The next time I played the local radio station which was basically an occasional country western song interspaced with commercials. I then asked for silence the last three times and I distracted myself by imagining myself singing solos again at church, humming the melody as I went through the scan. Imagining myself in choir practicing the Messiah helps as well.

I had a port put in but it was not done quite correctly and I could feel the tubing from it coiled up under the skin of my neck for the six months I had it. It developed a tunnel infection and had to be removed early.

When they hung the bags of chemo and attached my port, I marked in my journal whenever a new bag was hung and how my body reacted to it. I made it my prayer the chemo wouldn't kill me outright.

God is my refuge and my strength; He is very present when I am in trouble; therefore I will not fear, for he is with me. He was with me then; He is with me now. And he will be with you if you let Him.

"Peace comes not from the absence of trouble, but from the presence of God."

Alexander MacLaren

June 4 2020

Day Seventy-three

2 Corinthians 5:17
Therefore, if anyone is in Christ, he is a new creation; old things have passed away; behold, all things have become new.

I still remember it like yesterday and it's been over a dozen years ago, on a Tuesday, I was diagnosed with stage 3 Hodgkin's Lymphoma, a form of cancer that invades the lymphatic system. The doctor told me to stop work immediately and take medical leave. By the following Monday I was in the hospital getting a port set in. The next day, my chemo started. I hardly had time to breathe, let alone get used to the idea of being deathly ill. I couldn't get this sick, I had things to get done!

You see, I'd never taken care of myself, mostly others got all the attention. I thought I was just fine, but I allowed the stress of 'too much to do too soon' take over my life. I ended up weakening myself badly enough that this disease would claim my life for several months.

When you have cancer, you lose control and the medical folks take over, the medicine takes over, the treatments take over, and what you have left is a lot of time to think. You don't have the energy for much else.

And when I slowed down and started thinking and going over what my life had been and where I had been, I wasn't very happy with what I found out about myself. I was demanding and bossy and pushy; I had way too short a temper and I depended much too much on my intellect and not enough on my faith to pull me through bad situations. I made snap judgements too often and I expected instant response. It short, I looked myself over and realized I'd allowed myself to become one of those very efficient bitches that give womanhood a bad name. And Christian witness? Only if you thought Christ had a lot of deadlines and spent all His time tearing up the moneychangers in the temple and not enough time healing.

It's very humbling to ask God to show you your faults and then actually have Him do it. I had to take a deep breath and ask what to work on next, besides my cancer.

The cancer was just a symptom to slow me down; it took the eleven months of chemotherapy to lick the cancer; it took the eleven months of soul searching and getting closer to God to bring me to the realization I needed to become a new creature. I thought I was but I had only evolved into a meaner version of a pushed too far mom.

I had allowed the work of this job I lived to become my substitute for what was really important; I had to go back and allow God to do some real heart work on me to make me be what He wanted: kinder, more introspective and more apt to hear when He asked something of me. I had to lose my independent nature and become dependent on Him. I have been happier because of it. I wouldn't wish cancer on anyone; but if that is what it takes to help you become His new creation, then trust me, you can make it through and you can change.

> "Christ is a substitute for everything, but nothing is s substitute for Christ."
> Harry Ironside.

June 5 2020

Day Seventy-four

Psalm 119:165
"Great peace have those who love your law; nothing can make them stumble."

Have you ever had one of those moments when you thought nothing else could possibly go bad?

I went into a teaching hospital to have chemo started for lymphoma. I had been staged at just under a four level, which means it had already spread above and below my diaphragm.

As I was settled into my bed, trying not to be nervous, aware that the port which had been put in two days ago still was not healed completely, glued together, so to speak, a young nurse came in. She went over a permission to treat paper in great detail, how this treatment had side effects, some of them being

1) loss of hair
2) nausea
3) fatigue
4) easy bruising, slow clotting rate
5) anemia
6) constipation or diarrhea
7) rashes
8) mouth sores
9) pain

10) skin cracking
11) lung problems
12) possible instant death as some folks hearts won't take it and they had no idea to know who would live or die through the first treatment but if you made it through one, most likely you'd make it through all 20 treatments. They had it here instead of at my small home hospital in the event I was one of those.

Then she asked if I might want something for nerves. I told her no, signed the paper, leaned back and began to pray. I was going to be fine. Dan was parking the car and he'd be here to hold my hand. It was 11:00, check in time and it was supposed to start at 1. I had not eaten since I had been earlier warned of nausea and I hate throwing up.

Another student nurse came in, said basically the same thing, and asked I sign her paper.

Still another student came in, said the same thing, and asked I sign her paper.

Another student nurse came in asked what I'd had for lunch and when I told her I hadn't eaten, she said that wouldn't do at all, I needed to eat, "let me get you a menu because we wouldn't want you to think our hospital was one of those places where they don't feed people a last meal." Really! A last meal? It still sticks with me today, of course I laugh now, but back then…

Dan came in. He settled in to read a book. He got up to go to the bathroom because the sign on the door said the facilities in my room were only for the patient and he had to find one in the hallway for guests.

Fifteen minutes went by. A chaplain came in and asked if I wanted her to pray for me. I told her prayer was always welcome. She smiled, asked what denomination I came from and when I said I was a Seventh-day Adventist, her face blanched, she closed her book of prayers and said she hadn't any prayers for that religion and said I'd best call someone who could pray for me. She didn't return.

Have you ever had a time in your life when you really can't figure out what else to say to God? I mean, I'd repeated over and over, please let me stay patient; please let me live through this and if I don't let Dan find someone good to help him with the kids. And I hope it doesn't hurt too much. All that and variations of the same and I simply was exhausted from no food since six pm the night before, no liquids, little rest and plain out fear.

All together afterwards, I had counted by the time I actually got chemo eleven student nurses came in reading their forms to me so I could sign them. Sometimes, it does not pay to be too nice! And this hospital couldn't even pray for me because I was something they, or at least the chaplain, had not heard of before. I closed my eyes but you know, a hospital is a noisy place, and rest isn't that easy. And I'd run out of things to say to God. So I did the only thing I could do: I started to hum quietly all the hymns I could think of; and some of them started out pretty heavy but gradually they brightened up. I was humming "When I feel me going under, calm the waters ,Lord. When the storm is all around me, calm the sea. When I cry for help, Oh, hear me Lord and hold out your hand. Touch my life, heal the raging storm in me."

I learned a lesson that day. If you have no words, use someone else's; the words of hymns, the Bible verses you've learned, not your words, but His, and they help immeasurably,. When you're facing a crisis, when you can't think of the words, start to hum and let the words of others go across your mind. It soothes, it calms and it relaxes and it enables you to meet whatever it is you're meeting.

"God will meet you where you are in order to take you where He wants you to go."

Tony Evans

June 6 2030

Day Seventy-five

Psalm 118:24
"This is the day that the Lord has made; let us rejoice and be glad in it."

Dan came back and read. Time passed., The shift changed. Another student nurse came in, read the treatment papers and said she had to start my IV. I explained about the port. She looked surprised and left.

A regular nurse came in to take blood. She did not use the port, she just drew blood and left.

Time passed. Dan's stomach started to growl so I sent him downstairs for supper. I was brought a supper consisting or orange gelatin, weak tea(I don't drink tea), a hamburger (I'm a vegetarian) white bread (I don't eat white bread) margarine and coffee. There was a package of three Oreo cookies. I took those. No one had asked if I was a vegetarian. I rang to have the tray taken away. The nurse asked if I wasn't hungry. I explained the problem, she said it wasn't on her chart and she took the tray. I never did get supper.

Dan came back from his supper and two more student nurses came in. I'd now been waiting for four hours for a treatment that was supposed to be at 1. The nurses looked at the chart finally and discovered I wasn't allowed to eat until I'd had the first treatment and I'd been fasting all day and they made sure I hadn't eaten anything. (I'd saved the Oreos for after the treatment, hoping to get some milk to have with them, so the package was under my pillow.). I asked where the nurse was who was going to do the treatment and was told she wasn't even at the hospital yet! She'd had a family get together and wasn't supposed to come in today, but they'd called her to come and set this up and she was on her way. Then, like a Greek chorus, they went all over the same permission slip. And they asked me if I needed something to calm me down. I finally agreed and they came back quickly with 50 mg of Xanax. I hesitated. I asked how many other student nurses were on this shift and on being told six, I swallowed it.

The "real" oncology nurse came in and she had the same permission slip. I asked her why in the world I needed this again and she told me that all the student nurses had to have a certain number of permission slips for their field work and since I was one of the calm ones, they were all trying to get me since I didn't yell or anything. Student nurses are human and they had each told the next one that I was a good patient so…some people, it seems, get quite nasty about being reminded they could be dead in fifteen minutes…so I signed her slip.

Dan and I prayed as she went back to get the meds and I told him about the chaplain, we laughed and they started the chemo.

And I lived.

"God has a purpose behind every problem. He uses circumstances to develop our character. In fact, he depends more on circumstances to make us like Jesus than he depends on our reading the Bible."

Rick Warren

Day Seventy-six

Joel 2:12-13
"Now, therefore," says the LORD, "Turn to Me with all your heart, With fasting, with weeping, and with mourning." So rend your heart, and not your garments; Return to the LORD your God,

For He is gracious and merciful, Slow to anger, and of great kindness; And He relents from doing harm.

Have you had one of *those* days?

You go to make a pie for church potluck only to find someone found the bag of apples and either ate most of them or donated them to the local pet rabbits as treats.

You go to make cookies for the potluck and someone ate the chocolate chips and the peanut butter jar, empty of course, was placed nicely back on the shelf so you didn't know you needed peanut butter.

You decide, OK, no pie, no cookies make bread, plan B. You make a nice batch of homemade bread, it is ready to be made unto homemade rolls to put into pans and you spray Windex on the pan instead of PAM?

You toss out cooking as a bad job today and go out to your front garden to pick flowers for an arrangement and find your best rose bush has been attacked by Japanese beetles and now is literally a skeleton. Rather than make an elaborate three point arrangement of prickly stems, you decide this would be a good time to run out on errands and get away from the crazy that is your life, so you drive into town, go to the store, go gather up the cart full of food and go to check out, only to realize you not only left your money in the bank, but your checkbook is at home where you were just reconciling it this morning before you started baking.

You go home to get the checkbook, and your child, whom you love dearly, who was supposed to have been watched by husband who is deep into a baseball game, comes into the house and explains to great length just why it was important for her to wear her new dress and shoes outside in the mud to show the neighborhood kids who just happened to be playing frisbee, and the mud will come out before tonight's church program, right? The church program that's in less than two hours? And you still don't have any homemade bread or cookies to take, much less time to hand scrub out a dress marked gentle wash only, tumble dry . . . And your dear husband gave her permission to go out in this mess? Then he comes in with the nibbles and wants to know if we can have supper before we leave since he doesn't like to eat that late. So what's my dream for supper?

Oh, yes, if you are alive and living in this world, whether or not you have a family to take care of, you've had those days. And just when your nerves are on the last string, and you know you are about to give up and start throwing a mommy fit of major proportions, there's a still small voice inside telling you, "Return to me with all your heart...rend your heart and not your garments."

What? Now? Yes, return. It's the hardest thing to do sometimes, or it seems hard for the first three minutes. It's time to take a break, go into a private place and tell God about it. He is able to calm you, to listen to you, and to help you see the humor of the situation. He reminds you He saved you, you are His child, and He can't wait to take you and your family up here with Him where they don't have grocery stores or bank accounts.

In the meantime, you are loved, take a breath, and get on with life.

> "Saving us is the greatest and most concrete demonstration of God's love, the definitive display of his Grace though out time and eternity."
>
> David Jeremiah

June 8 2020

Day Seventy-seven

Psalm 34:18
"The Lord is near to the brokenhearted and saves the crushed in spirit."

My grandfather used to say that deaths in family's came in threes. He said it was like a pattern and I'd see it as I got older. I never really noticed it until three years ago when my only sister died first, alone at home. A year after that, my mother passed away and nine months later, my father. It seemed I could never quite finish grieving for one when the next passed.

As a pastoring family, my extended family asked us to do the services, so we really couldn't grieve much until afterwards: there was the service to prepare, and the people to contact. And after the services were over, and the dinner after, there was life to attend to and somehow, my grieving at each death got put off until the following Sabbath day.

With each of them, I spent a Sabbath sitting alone, going through mental pictures of the last things we had said, the last time we had talked, the last moments we shared, and remembering earlier, better times. Some thoughts brought a smile, some a tear, but being a Christian meant that I knew I would, with no shadow of doubt, see them again and just like when were separated at times here on earth, we'd sit and spend time catching up what had gone on.

That's one of the huge blessings in having the Lord as a member of my family; He has promised our grief will be short here; that we will see each other in the resurrection, and we will finally have time to sit, and visit and reminisce on the good times, the small problems here and catch up, not only with our loved ones, but with Him. Have you ever wondered what He's been doing since He left and sent His Spirit to tend to us? It will make for an interesting visit. And I really want to see my folks again, and some really close friends who went before and our Lord. Do you have the assurance that you will see your loved ones again?

"No two Christians will ever meet for the last time."

Unknown

Stories To Mold Your Worldview

Some final stories to cement the habit of God visiting!

Jun 9 2020

Day Seventy-eight

2 Chronicles 7:14
If my people who are called by my name humble themselves, and pray and seek my face and turn from their wicked ways, then I will hear from heaven and will forgive their sin and heal their land.

This verse was used during the national day of prayer. A song written by Michael Card, based on this verse has been used many times now and each time it seems more meaningful. Mr. Card is a theologian, a song writer and an example of a man using his talents the way God would see them used.

"Forgive oh Lord and heal our land
And give us eyes to seek Your face and hearts to understand
That You alone make all things new
And the blessings of the land we love are really gifts from You

If My people will humbly pray and seek My face and turn away
From all their wicked ways
Then I will hear them and move My hand
And freely then will I forgive and I will heal their land

Unite our hearts in one accord
And make us hungry for Your peace and burdened for the poor

> And grant us hope that we might see
> The future for the land we love our life our liberty"

(Michael Card, 1999)

The promise that God will heal our land if we turn back to him is one of the grandest in the Bible. The idea that God in His heaven cares enough to come down and bless this country if only we will turn away from our sins is one that cannot be ignored. If our politicians stop being self-centered and remember to pray; if our moms and dads and children will pray; if those who are actively in sin turn from their evilness, then He can bless us, make us great again, make us a guiding force in the world. By its very nature, there is a down side. If we don't turn back, He must withdraw and leave us. If we turn from Him, He has to turn from us.

If the heavens seem as if the sky has turned into a trampoline over us, bouncing back our prayers, could it be we have not turned our back on sin; we have not made Him the leader of our life.. Do we want our country to be great again? Then turn your hearts to Him.

Many, many years ago, when I was a child, I didn't understand what country meant. I thought country was simply what we called the property we lived on. As I became a teenager, I learned about nations and governments in civics class, and I still didn't understand completely. As I grew up, got married, had children, and set about my adult life, I was too busy to figure out what it meant to be a citizen. Yes, I voted, yes, I put my hand over the heart for the Pledge, and I loved the parades, but I still didn't comprehend what it meant to be an American. It came clear to my mind when life slowed down, when the husband and I finally got closer to an understanding of how our freedoms are eroding.

We remember how we took for granted that we could always speak our mind, attend the church of our choice, believe as we wished, vote, own a gun if we wanted. We didn't know what a privilege that sort of freedom actually was until we saw what others did not have; and how they were willing to march thousands of miles to try and get what we take for granted. I met people in college, students from foreign countries who were totally flabbergasted at our freedom of speech. I met along the way people who have state religions and who would be fined or even spend time in jail or executed for not believing as the state wishes. I thank God that there are still enough Christians in our great country that we are still fighting to keep our freedoms intact. People of other worldviews, other religions just don't get it. They've never had freedom so they don't know what can be lost.

Those of us who grew up in freedom know just how easy it would be to lose that freedom. Get involved. Pray for our country. Get active with your local government. Don't forsake worshipping God with others. Vote according to conscience and not propaganda. We need to stand for our country. Otherwise, it can't stand for us.

"It cannot be emphasized too strongly or too often that this great Nation was founded, not by religionists, but by Christians; not on religions, but on the Gospel of Jesus Christ."
                                            Patrick Henry

June 10 2020

Day Seventy-nine

John 17:3
And this is eternal life, that they may know You, the only true God, and Jesus Christ whom You have sent.

I learn so much now, from reading about the trials of others. This one has always astonished me, and humbled me.

With a sickening crash, the tunnel collapsed around the 5 men in Salem, Kentucky. The coal miners knew they were in big trouble if they could not dig out or be dug out.. They knew that each moment might be their last. They had very little food and only a trickle of dirty water they could catch in a cup. The possibility of further collapse was ever-present. They had only the light from one unbroken carbide lantern, and then darkness and dead silence, except for shifting rocks and occasional crashes in the distance. They were in deep trouble.

What would you do in that situation? All but one of them were married, and all had families they knew they might not see again. They were from 25 to 37 years old.

They could have cursed God for their bad luck, but they didn't. They could've given up hope and died, but they didn't. Instead, they prayed for each other and for their families, who they knew were outside waiting and praying, and each made a new commitment to God. Before the only light went out, and the darkness overtook their little hole, one man made a rough letter to the world, which he put in his headband. It said, "If we are dead when you find us, we are all saved in Christ." All of them signed it.

It was 153 hours before they were rescued. When the rescuers broke through to them, they found them praying for their families. As for the miners, first they were in total darkness, and they saw the most beautiful thing suddenly appear; the face of their rescuers by lantern-light.

All of us live in a world of darkness. We simply are too blind to see how dark this world is in reality. The only light and the only rescue is through a person – Jesus Christ. Knowing Him is the basis of our rescue from the world. He is our safe passage from this world of sin.

In a book I love to read called Desire of Ages, the author says, "As through Jesus we enter into rest, Heaven begins here. We respond to his invitation, come learn of me, and in thus coming, we begin the life eternal. Heaven is a ceaseless approaching to God through Christ" (p. 331).

Heaven starts with Him. Our rescue starts in Him and ends in Him. Ask Him to give you safe passage through the dark mines in your life. This part of our trip may seem gloomy, even frightening, but there is a light at the end of this tunnel. The shining up there in front of us? That's home.

> "The Christian life is not a constant high. I have my moments of deep discouragement. I have to go to God in prayer with tears in my eyes, and say, 'O God, forgive me,' or 'Help me.'"
>
> Billy Graham

June 10, 2020

Day Eighty

Galatians 6:10
"So then, as we have opportunity, let us do good to everyone, and especially to those who are of the household of faith."

I'm a mental health therapist, among other things, and often I tell my clients who are lonely, or out of sorts with their lives that the true key to their own happiness is serving others. When we take ourselves out of our own needs, and we give or act for others, our own problems seem very small.

I remember years ago, a young man came to me hurt and upset after breaking off his engagement. He felt he didn't have a reason to go on. I listened to his problems for an entire session and set another session. At the next session he began again in the same vein, but I interrupted him.

"I have heard how you've been wronged and hurt and I agree, it was terrible, horrible and you are in pain. But what have you done this week to change what's going on?"

"I can't possibly fall in love again." He expostulated. "I'm still bleeding."
"You don't understand what I mean," I said quietly.

I explained to him that when a person has been hurt, the best cure is to find someone else and help them over a tight spot. It can be a friend, it can be a stranger, but just the act of doing a Random Act of Kindness, a unpaid, simple thing, can raise your own endorphins(those are feel good hormones). I suggested that for this coming week, he needed to, among other things, just smile when he passed someone. That's all, just smile. The second bit of homework was to simply do one little thing for someone in his immediate family they don't expect. I wanted him to report just those things the next week.

The following week, he came in and grinned as he reported smiling at other folks seemed to make them smile back. And he had picked some flowers out of the yard and out them on the kitchen table so when his widowed dad came home from work, he found them there on the kitchen table. His dad's reaction of surprise and joy at the flowers lifted his own spirits and he thought it might be good to be nicer to some of the folks at work.

He started remembering the manners he'd been taught, just smiling at folks and thanking them when he really didn't feel like it and finally found out he did feel like it. He was well on the way out of his sadness and into a better attitude towards life. And when he later found another young lady and they decided to wed, I was invited to the wedding....being kind to others comes back as a kindness to ourselves.

He said "Love...as I have loved you." We cannot love too much. "

Amy Carmichael

June 1, 2020

Day Eighty-one

Jeremiah 29:11
"For I know the plans I have for you, declares the Lord, plans for welfare and not for evil, to give you a future and a hope."

Becoming a Social worker requires internships at differing agencies to learn a little more about the many and varied kinds of work being done. I worked for some time at an agency called Hospice. Hospice is an agency that specializes in the treatment of the terminally ill. Most of the people who come to Hospice have less than 6 months to live. Most have cancer, AIDS or some debilitating disease. Hospice does all it can to relieve them of pain and to help them get their affairs in order for death. It may sound gloomy, but it isn't at all. The people there have a dedication to others that is beautiful to see. Of all the people I ever worked with they were the most optimistic. They loved the people they worked with, and it showed in their smiles and gentleness and attention to detail.

One of the things that those who work with the clients of Hospice do is to help the grieving family. They go with them to the funeral and they counsel them for the first year and help them get through the stages of grief.

I attended several funerals as a volunteer and could not help seeing the difference between a Christian funeral and other funerals. At Christian funerals, the pastor speaks of hope and the Second coming; of babies being flown back to their mother's arms, of wives holding their husbands in their arms once again. Even though there are tears, there is hope.

On the other hand, in an unbeliever's funeral, the emphasis is entirely on feeling better, getting through it, because you won't ever see your loved on again. They have no hope. For them, the funeral really means never seeing their loved ones again. They cry tears of agony and the pain of separation. They know this is the absolute end. The stages of grief sometimes become complicated, hard to go through, the finality throws people into real depression. It's hard to see, and difficult to watch.

Do you have friends who don't know the hope we have? Have pity on them! Tell them about our hope. You are God's mouthpiece. Don't they deserve your help? On this journey we are on, this life path, one of our goals needs to be relieving the pain all around us. In doing this, we lessen the sum total of sadness in this world.

For those who want to understand better how to deal with the natural grief that occurs at the death of a loved one, although there is some disagreement, most of the experts agree with Elizabeth Kubler-Ross original list as being a very fair approximation of how we as people grieve. The stages of grief are:

Denial: in our heads we say "This can't be happening !"

Anger: We think "This is not fair! Someone needs to fix this!"

Bargaining: we try to work a way out of it, "If you will just fix this, just don't let him/her be dead, please make it stop."

Depression: the stage in which we finally realize nothing is going to change and we start to cry, weep, and feel terribly sad.

Acceptance: After the depression starts to lift, and we know this cannot change, we accept it. We are still sad, but we know we will go on. We start going back to our regular lives.

Even Christians go through these stages, but they aren't linear, as such. In the worldview of the Christian, we know we will see our loved ones again. Death becomes more like a long trip they took ahead of us, and someday we will join them, and someday, we will be together in a place where we will never part again. Death is no longer a victorious enemy we all face: it becomes simply another stage in life on earth, and one which is not final. If you are walking the path of loss right now, take heart. He is with you and never leaves even when life seems the darkest.

"When we lose one blessing, another is often most unexpectedly given in its place."
C.S. Lewis

June 12 2020

Day Eighty-two

Psalm 19:12
"But who can discern their own errors? Forgive my hidden faults."

All of us have things within us that we'd really not want other people to know about. We're not exactly ashamed but we get this queasy feeling when we think about them. We resolve to stop that hidden thing, that secret fault, but every now and then, it raises up like Lazarus and reminds us that we're all too human, all too weak, and all too prone to slip up.

With me, it's worry. I had a friend once send me a funny little poster that showed a grandma with her hands on her hips saying. "Of course I worry about stuff that may not happen. The fact they don't happen shows that worrying works." I had to smile at that. It's not that it's wrong to worry about the 'actually this is a big thing problems' (for instance, I've just lost my job, how am I going to survive? Or My child is very ill and the doctors are not being encouraging about her chances) but to make up a problem to worry about (What if a meteor hits the earth? What if I'm driving down the interstate and a semi runs over my car?) that most likely won't happen, that's the kind of worry we are approaching here.

I had to find some way to get a handle on the worry bug I carried around, especially since so many of my own clients had it as well, to find it and crush it out of my subconscious mind. As I have learned to do, when worried about something, do some research and prove it can't happen. So I started studying worry and found some fascinating things about worrying in the United States:

- When you worry too much, your body actually misreads smells and everything smells bad.

- Worriers often have problems with their balance. They sometimes feel dizzy for no apparent reason and sway more than others while standing normally.

- Chronic worrying can affect you so much that it interferes with your appetite, lifestyle habits, relationships, sleep, and job performance.
- Worrying induces your body to produce cortisol. Cortisol compromises your immune system. As a result, you will become more susceptible to disease.
  Researchers have also found a relationship between cortisol and diabetes, osteoporosis, and heart disease.

In my research I found many tools to aid me in my mission to stomp out worrying,. The best one was simply to write down what was worrying me, put the paper away in a drawer and not allow myself to think about the worry until a certain time that day; in others words, set up a specific worry time. Take all the slips from that day out at say, nine pm and look at them. Ask three questions:

1. Is this something I can do anything about really?
2. If it is, what plan can I make to fix it tomorrow morning?
3. If it isn't, tell God to take care of it, I can't and then burn it, or tear it into little pieces and throw it away.

If the worry comes back and rears its head, simply repeat, I have already dealt with you. I have better things to do with what I can change., No reason to continue with this one. There are plenty of things to work on without worrying about the ones I can do nothing about. I have a plan; I will follow that.

For the Christian, worrying is not always a lack of faith, but a simple fault that needs to be mended and dealt with; so ask God to help you sort out what is a real thing you need to be concerned about and what can simply be sent away as not relevant to you. He is there, He can help you change your hidden faults and help you become stronger on your travels here on earth. He can help you through any hidden faults; He will even point them out if you ask Him. Then once you know them, He helps you fix them.

"God grades on the Cross not on the curve."
Adrian Rogers

Day Eighty-three

Isaiah 29:19
"The meek shall obtain fresh joy in the Lord, and the poor among mankind shall exult in the Holy One of Israel."

"Emily, why do you always wear white clothes?"
"I prefer them."
"Why don't you go out? You'll never meet a man that way."
"I don't really want to meet a man. I have clothes and food and flowers. That's enough."
"That Emily Dickinson is so strange!"

Emily Dickinson was a private person. Born in Amherst, Massachusetts to an educated family, she wrote over 3000 beautiful poems in her life but no one saw them until after her death in 1886. No one knows why.

At age 23, she became a recluse and never left her home again. She wrote letters to her friends but never went out, not to weddings, not to funerals, not to go shopping. If she went out at all, it was to walk in the fields behind their house or to work in her flower garden but not to see people. She just didn't seem comfortable around people. But strangely she loved people. And she wrote for people, verses they would never read until after her death.

Many of Emily's poems are about God and nature. She had faith in her heavenly Father's care and an almost whimsical love for nature. After her death, her poems were published and were received with great acclaim. She is recognized as one of America's greatest poets. Perhaps we can learn most about Ms. Dickerson by reading her poems. Here's some of her short poems which I like very much:

> I never saw a moor
> I never saw the sea
> Yet I know how the heather looks
> And what a wave must be.
> I never spoke with God'
> Nor visited in heaven
> Yet certain am I of the spot
> As if a chart were given.

Another poem I really enjoy is simply titled Farewell

> Tie the strings to my life, my Lord,
> Then I am ready to go!
> Just a look at the horses --
> Rapid! That will do!
>
> Put me in on the firmest side,
> So I shall never fall;
> For we must ride to the Judgment,
> And it's partly downhill.
>
> But never I mind the bridges,
> And never I mind the sea;
> Held fast in everlasting race
> By my own choice and thee.
>
> Good-by to the life I used to live,
> And the world I used to know;
> And kiss the hills for me, just once;
> Now I am ready to go!

And yet another poem, a favorite among most teens I know…

       I'm nobody! Who are you?
Are you nobody, too?
Then there's a pair of us -- don't tell!
They'd banish us -- you know!

How dreary to be somebody!
How public like a frog
To tell one's name the livelong day
To an admiring bog!

Emily's poems bring us comfort and help us understand God's love better. Someday I want to talk to Emily in a world where she won't need to be shy anymore. If you are shy, if you think you contribute nothing, think of this retiring poet. Her works have spanned the globe and it's only in heaven she'll even know how much good she has done.

Success is on the same road as failure; success is just a little further down the road.
                               Jack Hyles

Day Eighty-four

2 Corinthians 5:17
"Therefore, if anyone is in Christ, he is a new creation. The old has passed away; behold, the new has come."

Neither of my folks ever graduated from high school. Both were children of the Depression, and dad was pulled out of school at age 12 to go to work. His first job was in a corn field, hoeing, having to keep up with adults, hoeing ten hours a day for a dollar day. He was allowed to keep ten cents of every dollar. His mom got a quarter of each dollar to help with food; his dad took the rest.

At fourteen he was working in the coal mines.

My mom got to eleventh grade: she loved to read. But they were so poor, so desperately poor, living as share farmers, mom heard of a job cleaning a rich lady's house part time. She became a maid; at one time she worked as a maid for three different houses. She gave half her money to her mother; she saved half of the rest and kept the other half. She says she saved up and had her hair done. It cost a dollar and she felt wonderful to have her hair actually styled. She bought her own clothes, she paid her bus fare into town.

Both of my parents always regretted never having gotten an education, Their entire lives they were hardworking, careful of their funds. My dad used to love to go to auctions and he'd buy boxes of books among other things so mom and the rest of us would have things to read. He wanted us to all have the things he couldn't have.

When I went to college the first time, I bombed out completely. I did not know how to study, how to learn. I was away from home for the first time and I was scared to death. My dad wanted one of us to go into the medical field so I went to a medical college. Big error; I had no background in medical ideas. I lasted two semesters and all that I did right was meet my husband. I went home, got a job as a nurse's aide, and Dan and I courted long distance.

We got married, had kids, and then when our economy crashed, we went back to school to retool and sharpen our abilities so we could get good jobs. I got through my undergraduate school with no problems; I got an excellent job and then I went back to university to get my Master's. That's where I met a certain professor who made the statement that no way would I ever be able to complete my degree. I proved him wrong, graduating with honors. My mom and dad were so proud of me. They didn't understand what I did for a living, but they were proud.

In this life, sometimes we are surrounded by nay-sayers; people who tell us that just because we (fill in whatever here, female, a minority, too young, too old whatever) we can't possibly achieve a goal we have set. My parents were handicapped by lack of education, but they raised four good citizens, they broke out of the cycle of poverty and into middle class, they did good in the world. I was born of uneducated, Appalachian parents.

Statistically, I should have failed to become what I wanted to be.

But God is good; He enables. He gave me courage when no one around me believed I could succeed.

I fought my insecurities and attained my goal. You can do that, too. You can push past the negative folks in your life and push forward in God's strength to do whatever He has suggested you do. Just because you fail once does not mean you will fail again; I failed when I followed someone else's dream for me. When I followed what God put in my path, I succeeded. You will too.

"As the flower turns to the sun, that the bright beams may aid in perfecting its beauty and symmetry, so should we turn to the Sun of Righteousness, that Heaven's light may shine upon us, that our character may be developed in to the likeness of Christ."
Ellen G. White

June 15 2020

Day Eighty-Five

James 1:22-27

"But be doers of the word, and not hearers only, deceiving yourselves. For if anyone is a hearer of the word and not a doer, he is like a man who looks intently at his natural face in a mirror. For he looks at himself and goes away and at once forgets what he was like. But the one who looks into the perfect law, the law of liberty, and perseveres, being no hearer who forgets but a doer who acts, he will be blessed in his doing. If anyone thinks he is religious and does not bridle his tongue but deceives his heart, this person's religion is worthless."

I do so love the Book of James. It's so practical. In fact, I read once it was so practical it was nearly left out of the canon of the Bible as being too pragmatic, too prosaic, more like instructions that spiritual.

It is so strange to me how people in general have decided that the verse above is about judgement. It's not; it's about love. If you truly love someone, you want to be with them: you want to stay with them, to do things for them, to bring a smile to their faces.

If you love God, you obey Him, not because it's a law but because He asked you to. Are you saved by good works? Of course not, but if you know that feeding the homeless, or being kind to a neighbor or helping a lost kid in the grocery store is something that will make God proud of you, like any good child, you do those things.

I remember when my kids were small, they wanted to do nice things for mommy. Forgetting the rule about not picking the flowers in the flower beds out front, one day two of them waded right into a patch of asters, picking flowers, breaking stems, stomping other flowers but proudly came to the house bearing gifts. I knew exactly where the flowers came from, thanked them for their flowers but took them out to the flower bed and showed them again the damage they had done, then showed them flowers they could pick without a problem.

God is like that; He's gentle but He has some rules to follow. We can do anything within the scope of those rules and He is pleased. The fields are wide with what we can do. Do we really want to kill someone, or steal or lie? I should hope not!

Our love for Him keeps us from those things; but it also should lead us to do those things He did while here, things not specified as needing to be done; acts showing kindness, showing love to others in His name. It's not difficult to be a child of God; He is in big things and little things, and He loves us so much. Our actions show whether or not we love Him as well.

"Forgive me for being so ordinary while claiming to know so extraordinary a God."

Jim Elliot

Day Eighty-Six

Revelation 20:10; 21:1, 3, 4
"And the devil that deceived them was cast into the lake of fire and brimstone . . . And I saw a new heaven and a new earth . . . Behold, the tabernacle of God is with men, and he will dwell with them, and God shall wipe away all tears from their eyes . . . for the former things are passed away."

These last verses in the Bible are so encouraging to me. The picture is of the earth made new for us, all the sin wiped away, the devil and his minions destroyed, gone forever; God's own palace/temple/castle comes down from God in heaven and settles in on this little planet, and He Himself wiping the tears from our eyes., and promising, guaranteeing there will be no more sorrow, or crying or hurting; no more cancer, or heart disease, or car accidents, no more stillborn babies, no more divorce or murder or killing; no more locked doors, no pets dying. All that is gone, passed away.

Such a magnificent promise! If you have ever lost someone, if you have ever been ill, if you are apparent worrying about their kids, if you are single and wished you weren't so lonely, none of that will be there. You will have a home with God Himself. Your sadness here will be gone in moment.

I am an author, sometimes I like to think over the verses on heaven in the Scriptures and let my imagination take over, wondering what my mansion will be like, if I can have hummingbirds live nearby, if I'll have a pet dolphin. Will I be able to dive deep and see the corals without a tank? What will space travel be like? Will we get up a lunch date with old friends and decide to go to a planet that has real unicorns and rainbow encased waterfalls? Will I and my angel plant a special garden with a silver bench just for visiting dignitaries, like Eve and Esther and Job?

When I speak to people down here, they can talk for hours about places they'd like to see, things they'd like to do here. When I ask them what's the first thing they want to do in heaven, they either say they want to ride a lion or eat fruit. Ok, fine, I like lions. Yet Scripture hints of so much more. No wars, no sin, no temptation any more. No thorns on roses. No biting insects. No flat tires, no poisonous snakes.

Just making a list of all the things sin has done to this world and their repair would take hours to contemplate, but the home in heaven is so much more. It's a hoe we go to with Jesus and we never can be kicked out; it's a home you can return to and it's always there, no roads get put over it, no dam floods it, no fire burns it. Best of all, those you love are there and you never will leave them again.

Yes the rainbow jewel walls will be beautiful, the golden streets and the tree of life sublime; but to hug my mom again, to laugh with my sister, to tell dad all of what went on after he died that will be heaven. And while we're hugging, our four angels will be smiling, and then leading us to visit with God. To touch the hand of God; to see his face, to know it was worth it all just to be here. That will be heaven.

"Surely it is not wrong for us to think and talk about Heaven. I like to find out all I can about it. I expect to live there through all eternity. If I were going to dwell in any place in this country, if I were going to make it my home, I would inquire about its climate, about the neighbors I would have — about everything, in fact, that I could learn concerning it. If soon you were going to emigrate, that is the way you would feel. Well, we are all going to emigrate in a very little while. We are going to spend eternity in another world. ... Is it not natural that we should look and listen and try to find out who is already there and what is the route to take?"
    D.L. Moody

Day Eighty-seven

Romans 1:16-17

"For I am not ashamed of the gospel of Christ, for it is the power of God to salvation for everyone who believes, for the Jew first and also for the Greek. For in it the righteousness of God is revealed from faith to faith; as it is written, "The just shall live by faith."

What is righteousness? When I've asked my friends and colleagues that question, I've gotten a variety of answers. One says it's right doing, Another that it's love. I've been told that righteousness is obeying the law, or is holiness. I tell them they have all missed the point of Scripture. Righteousness is nothing more and nothing less than Jesus.

Let's think this through together.

If righteousness was right doing, then why would you need Jesus? No, no need for a suffering Savior because you could earn your way to heaven. The Jains of India, who sweep the floor in front of them as they walk for fear of stepping on a bug, and who wear masks to avoid swallowing small life forms and killing something, would make it to heaven before most other people.

If righteousness is just love, then any happily married couple would be righteous. Bonnie and Clyde, the infamous bank robbers, or Nero and Octavia, the Roman despots would be easily eligible.

If righteousness could be had by merely obeying the law, most judges and lawyers should make it, because they really know the law, and they should be able to keep it to the letter.

If it were perfect holiness, we would all be lost. I haven't met any really holy people, have you? I've met good people. I've met kind people, but I haven't met many people who, in themselves, were naturally holy.

But if righteousness is Jesus, then we can be righteous, through Him. As long as we have Jesus as Savior, we can be righteous. The only way to find true righteousness is in Jesus. We know that, "all our righteousnesses *are* like filthy rags" (Is 64:6). We are incapable of righteousness in ourselves.

Morris Venden, one of my favorite writers, explains it this way. "Righteousness equals Jesus. Mankind plus Jesus equals righteousness. Mankind minus Jesus equals nothing." We are nothing without Him. We are everything with Him. When we accept Him, we become righteous. If we refuse him, we are nothing. Heaven is waiting for a people who have Christ's righteousness within them. Does he live in your mind today?

> "Night and day I pondered until I saw the connection between the justice of God and the statement that 'the just shall live by his faith.' Then I grasped that the justice of God is that righteousness by which through grace and sheer mercy God justifies us through faith. Thereupon I felt myself to be reborn and to have gone through open doors into paradise."
> Martin Luther

Day Eighty-eight

John 16:3
"These things I have spoken to you, that in Me you may have peace. In the world you will have tribulation; but be of good cheer, I have overcome the world."

The peace of God – is that simply a dream we have?

An old song my dad used to sing while working in his garage comes to mind, "Make the world go away, get it off of my shoulder . . ."(Eddie Arnold, 1966, and my dad, who I think did it better.)

Unfortunately, the world doesn't go away, and those of us who work in heaven's embassy – for that is what the church is here on this old world – seem to be under special attack sometimes.

Ever since Adam and Eve gave the devil control of this planet, those of us left here who are faithful to God are ambassadors to the lost, and our home is actually heaven, not here.

It can be comforting to think of the peace of God as being here within us. As we see the sickness, the pain, and the suffering that sin has caused everyone, and when we are wounded ourselves in the daily battles, it is good to know that this is temporary, and that He will give us His peace while we work.

I think that sometimes that the peace of God is like a wisp of fog within us: it hangs and envelopes our minds and helps us to feel rested. If we fight it, it leaves; if we accept it, it's there, surrounding and cooling us from the heat of our daily tasks. You can't put your fingers on it, or pick it up, or fill a bowl with it, but it fills you within.

On those days when so much seems to be bad in the world, the thought of a cooling bit of mist feels relaxing, like the cool just before twilight in the summer, or the early morning breezes. It refreshes us, it gives us energy and it sends us on our way, thinking of the care of Our Lord.

"A life in Christ is a life of restfulness. There may be no ecstasy of feeling, but there should be an abiding, peaceful trust. Your hope is not in yourself; it is in Christ. Your weakness is united to His strength, your ignorance to His wisdom, your frailty to His enduring might . . . Let the mind dwell upon His love, upon the beauty, the perfection of His character. . . "

Ellen G. White

Day Eighty-nine

Romans 8:6
"For to be carnally minded is death, but to be spiritually minded is life and peace".

"Church people" have a real problem.

You've probably seen it. We are so good! We don't drink, smoke, do drugs, live fast, dress wrong, use too much makeup or jewelry, we pay tithe, we go to church, we exercise, we sleep right, we do good, we support the right causes – and many of us are probably lost.

You see, living a good, moral life will not save you. You will not make yourself righteous by hard work. Sure, you won't fry your brain, you might live longer, you'll be less prone get cancer, but you'll burn just as long as any other sinner if you don't get right with God.

What consolation will it be to know you behaved yourself if you're lost?

If you live a moral life, you won't go to jail. You'll probably live a long time, and have a respected role in your community. But most likely, you will not be happy.

You see, you will always have an empty spot inside you. There will be a longing, a desire for something intangible. You will run as fast as you can to do and achieve and gain, and will fail just at the end of your journey.

The only thing that will cure the ache within is Christ's righteousness. The only thing that will save you is your relationship with Him. Anything else is just frivolity and time wasting. Being moral will not bring you righteousness, but righteousness from Christ will make you over and make you truly moral. Righteousness is found in a person. And that person is Jesus.

I am trying here to prevent anyone saying the really foolish thing that people often say about Him: "I'm ready to accept Jesus as a great moral teacher, but I don't accept his claim to be God". That is the one thing we must not say. A man who was merely a man and said the sort of things Jesus said would not be a great moral teacher. He would either be a lunatic — on the level with the man who says he is a poached egg — or else he would be the Devil of Hell. You must make your choice. Either this man was, and is, the Son of God, or else a madman or something worse. You can shut him up for a fool, you can spit at him and kill him as a demon or you can fall at his feet and call him Lord and God, but let us not come with any patronizing nonsense about his being a great human teacher. He has not left that open to us. He did not intend to. "

C. S. Lewis

June 20 2020

Day Ninety

John 12:*26*
If anyone serves Me, let him follow Me; and where I am, there My servant will be also. If anyone serves Me, him My Father will honor.

What an honor it is to serve God!

By serving him, we accomplish many things: we build our faith, and that of those who we encounter, we build our trust in Him; and we show the world that it is possible to follow God. It is more than figuratively being a light or salt or what have you; it's real.

Remember the story of the Velveteen rabbit?
'Real isn't how you are made,' said the Skin Horse. 'It's a thing that happens to you. When a child loves you for a long, long time, not just to play with, but REALLY loves you, then you become Real.'

'Does it hurt?' asked the Rabbit.

'Sometimes,' said the Skin Horse, for he was always truthful. 'When you are Real you don't mind being hurt.'

'Does it happen all at once, like being wound up,' he asked, 'or bit by bit?'

'It doesn't happen all at once,' said the Skin Horse.

'You become. It takes a long time. That's why it doesn't happen often to people who break easily, or have sharp edges, or who have to be carefully kept. Generally, by the time you are Real, most of your hair has been loved off, and your eyes drop out and you get loose in the joints and very shabby. But these things don't matter at all, because once you are Real you can't be ugly, except to people who don't understand."

(Margery Williams Bianco, <u>The Velveteen Rabbit</u>)

Sometimes the people of God may look worn, or tired, but they have an inner glow, a joy in life, that grows out of their love for Him and for others.

The story is told of the founder of the Salvation Army. He had just enough means to send a one word telegram to his struggling workers. His chosen word? "Others."

We love God by our work for Others. Not that it saves us, not that it perfects us, but because we are real, and as Real Christians, we cannot help but serve and love and give, just as Christ did before us. It is an honor and a privilege to serve Him.

Salvation is the free gift of God; it results in service to Him and to His others.

"You will find all of theology summed up in these two short sentences: Salvation is all of the grace of God; damnation is all of the will of man."

Charles Spurgeon

A Final Word

Our ninety day experiment has come to its close, and if you have read daily you will have developed a habit that will stay with you all your life; as long as you feed your heart daily in His word; as long as you remember your appointment, you will grow closer to He who loves us all and waits patiently for the time He will return to take us all to be with Him.

Thank you so for reading this little book, written for the glory of God. I hope you will take the time to go to God, if you haven't already, and take advantage of His free gift. Your prayer does not have to be fancy. It can be something as simple as this:

Dear God, I know that I am a sinner and there is nothing that I can do to save myself. I confess my complete helplessness to forgive my own sin or to work my way to righteousness. At this moment I trust Christ alone as the One who bore my sin when He died on the cross. I believe that He did all that will ever be necessary for me to stand in your holy presence. Thank you for sending your Son to die in my place. I am grateful that He has promised to accept me just as I am right now. Father, I take you at your word. I believe you are my Lord and Creator and God. Thank you for the assurance that you will walk with me through all my life and even my death. Thank you for hearing this prayer and making me your child. Lead me in the way you would have me go from this time forward.. In Jesus' Name. Amen.

If you pray this prayer, or one like it, please contact me and let me know. I'd love to send you some information to help you on your new life path.

My webpage address is: Travelerpelton.com

My facebook is travelerpelton

While you're there, I hope you take the time to get acquainted with us, the writers at Potpourri Publishing – because now we are members of the family of God, and I'd love to meet you!

And remember my invitation; when we get to heaven, at that last day, you'll find the tree of life spanning the river of life. The first Sabbath, I will be Jesus and the Father and my angel celebrating my first Sabbath in heaven. The second Sabbath, I will be with my family, all the generations back, again, celebrating,. But that next Sabbath is for all of us. On the third Sabbath after we get there, we're all meeting on the left bank for a potluck and to share our stories. We'd be pleased if you'd join us there. It's going to be grand! I can't wait to meet all of you. May God bless.

Promised Book Suggestions to continue your walk...

I promised you a list of books I have found useful in my own walk with God. I am quite eclectic: I read from authors of all faith persuasions for I feel we can all learn from each other. I am a practicing Seventh-day Adventist; that does not keep me from reading and absorbing the good in others. Here are some books you may find helpful:

First of all, and foremost is the Bible. I enjoy the Peshitta translation by Lamsa, The New King James and once in a while one of the modern paraphrases. I found reading the Chronological Bible fascinating, as it puts it all in historical order, instead of its usual order and it fixes better in your mind just what periods things occurred. Whichever is your favorite, reading it each day is important. Start in one of the gospels if you are new to it, I would suggest Luke, and read each day until you have learned something new. I don't know how many times I have gone through the Bible: I've been reading it since I was 12 or 14 and got the first one that was mine. I always see something new each time. Other books of interest:

By Max Lucado
- Six Hours One Friday,
- When God Whispers Your Name
- 3:16 The Numbers of Hope
- Unshakable Hope

By Philip Yancy

- The Jesus I Never Knew
- What's So Amazing About Grace?
- Where Is God When It Hurts?

By Morris Venden

- Obedience by Faith
- Love God and Do as You Please
- Modern Parables
- Your Friend, The Holy Spirit
- 95 Thesis on Righteousness' by Faith

Clifford Goldstein

- Life Without Limits

CS Lewis

- The Screwtape Letters
- Mere Christianity
- The Problem of Pain
- And for fun-The Chronicles of Narnia

Chuck Swindoll

- Improving Your Serve
- Growing Strong in the Seasons of Life
- Living Beyond the Daily Grind

Lee Strobel

- The Case for Christ

Ellen G. White
- Steps to Christ

- Christ's Object Lessons
- The Sanctified Life

Francis Schaeffer
- How Then Should We Live?
- A Christian Manifesto

Philip Keller
- A Shepherd Looks at Psalm 23
- Sky Edge
- Sea Edge
- Lessons from a Sheep Dog

Johnathan Cahn
- The Harbinger
- The Mystery of Shemitah
- The Paradigm

Is that all of the good books? Oh, my, no! This is just the start of wonderful appointments with God, each day learning as you read, leaning a little closer to Him.

Suggested Scriptures for daily meditation:
- Psalm 91
- Psalm 46
- Revelation 21 and 22
- Psalms 1:1-3
- Philippians 4:8
- Matthew 6:26-30

My Prayer Requests Of God

Date   request

May 9 '20   ❀   <u>For Stacy to come home to her family</u>
                 For my Family to be whole Again

May 11 '20   ❀   <u>I pray that everyone believing Gay life is</u>
                 godly will see the light & return to the fold.

May 12   ❀   <u>Please help me be faithful at work & do</u>
                 in unto you

His Answers to my Requests

Date   reply

My Prayer Requests Of God

Date request

His Answers to my Requests

Date   reply

My Prayer Requests Of God

Date request

His Answers to my Requests

Date   reply

My Prayer Requests Of God

Date   request

❀ _____

❀ _____

❀ _____

❀ _____

❀ _____

❀ _____

❀ _____

❀ _____

❀ _____

❀ _____

❀ _____

❀ _____

❀ _____

His Answers to my Requests

Date   **reply**

❀ _____

❀ _____

❀ _____

❀ _____

❀ _____

❀ _____

❀ _____

❀ _____

❀ _____

❀ _____

❀ _____

❀ _____

❀ _____

And I thought to let you in on another devotional book we have just put out for families to share with their children called <u>Lenten Stories for God's Little Children.</u> It can be used at any time of the year for family worship; or simply as good short bedtime stories that teach your little ones about Him.

Here's one of them we thought you'd enjoy.

Splitting Skins

"Hey, Mom! Look what I found in the old shoe!" called Emmy.

"What old shoe?" Mother sounded a bit worried.

"Down in the creek. Grandpa said he used to love creeks when he was little, so while you were shopping, he took us to the creek to babysit us. I found this old shoe and when I dumped it out, I caught him. Isn't he neat?"

Mother peeked inside the jar Emmy was holding. Inside was a three inch crawfish, moving slowly, holding up its' front claws defensively.

Daddy came in. "Hey, that's great! Let's put him in the aquarium.

"I don't think it's very healthy, Dan," objected Mother. "He moves so slow. I've caught enough crawfish to know that they move fast, normally."

"I didn't know you caught crawfish, Mom," and said Emmy in surprise.

"I was a kid once, too, and we lived on a farm with a creek and I've caught my share of critters." She looked at it again. "I don't know if it can carry diseases to the tropical fish or not. You sure you want it in the aquarium with the guppies?"

"It's worth a try, Mother," said Daddy. "I'll put some medication in the water to help prevent any illness."

Daddy dumped the creature into the aquarium, where it slithered down under a group of rocks.

"Look at all those legs!" exclaimed Beni from one side of the aquarium.

"It looks awesome, all right," said Daddy. "Look at that, he's got more than one pair pinchers."

"Why don't you go look up crayfish in the field guide on pond life and see what the thing eats?" suggested Mother. "Try to find out how big it's going to get too."

The next morning, Beni called, "Daddy! Come quick! Something is wrong with the crawfish!"

Daddy came over to the tank. The crawfish was bending itself double and reaching back with his claws and rubbing himself frantically.
"Maybe he has fleas," said Miah. He had given his dog, Shadow, a flea bath the day before.

"Don't believe they can get fleas," said Emmy. "They're cold blooded. Do you think the guppies are bothering him?"

"They're a lot smaller than he is," said Mother. "Let's go eat breakfast. We'll check on him after."

Breakfast didn't take very long, for everyone wanted to see what was happening to the new creature. Beni got there first and yelled, "Daddy come quick! His back is busted open and his insides are coming out!"

Everyone ran for the aquarium. After looking for a moment, Daddy said, "Oh, is that all that's happening? This is normal behavior. He's splitting the old shell and climbing out of it. That's how they grow. See, their skeletons are on the outside of them. When the inside gets too big for the outside, they grow new skin underneath, shed the outside skin and come out bigger. It's just growing, that's all."

"That's why he was so slow," said Mother. "He was getting ready to grow." Everybody watched as the crawfish slowly extricated himself from his shell. Finally, he was through. He washed himself all over, and then walked away from the old shell. Daddy took a net and took the old shell out for them to study.

"He must be three 1/two inches long now," said Fawn.

"I'm sure glad I don't have to split my skin to grow," said Emmy. "He even had to pull out his arms and pincers and stuff. I wonder if it hurt?"

"From the way he was acting while he was shedding, I think he must've been uncomfortable," said Daddy. "Just look how complex even a simple little garbage cleaner-upper is. This is just one of God smaller creatures. But look at intricately he is made."

"And all God had to do was say, 'let there be creepy crawly things,' and they were all here," said Fawn.

"I'm glad God made crawfish," said Emmy. "I wonder what else I can find in Grandpa's Creek? Can I go to Grandpa's house, Mom?"

"No, one critter is enough for this week," said Mother. "If you catch anything else, study it, but let it go. It will be happier free. Let's get our chores done. Then you can go and show Grandpa the crawdad's shell. It ought to be dry enough by then."

God's Love Reminder Verse:
So that I may boldly say, the Lord is my helper, and I will not fear what man shall do to me. (Hebrews 13:6)

About the Author:

J. Traveler Pelton was born in West Virginia in the last century. She served as Nation's Mother for her tribe, for six years: she is wife to Dan (45 years!), mother of six adults, a grandmother of eight, a Clinically Licensed Independent Social Worker with Supervisory Status, at present in private practice, a retired adjunct professor of social work at her local university and an
insatiable reader. She is a cancer survivor. Traveler avidly studies science and technology, fascinated by the inventiveness of people. She is quick to draw parallels in different fields and weave stories around them. Traveler is a fabric artist and her most enjoyable time is
spent spinning yarn while spinning yarns for the grandkids…

You can reach Traveler at her website: travelerpelton.com

Or like us and share us on Facebook at Traveler Pelton
Or write to her by snail mail at
Springhaven Croft
212 Sychar Rd.
Mt. Vernon, OH 43050

She loves to hear from her readers!
All our books are available on Amazon as both eBook and print copy, Kindle unlimited as free downloads

We'd love it if you'd leave us a review! It helps others find our books.

Your Attention Please!!!!
Would you like to join the team at Potpourri Books?
Traveler is always looking for responsible beta readers for her new books. A beta reader gets a prepublication copy of all new books, free of charge in exchange for an honest review written on Amazon, and a short email letting her know of any glitches you may have found that got past the editor, any suggestions you may have, and your opinion of the book. What else do you get out of it?
A beta reader gets:
A free download of one of her already published books and
as soon as your review of that book gets placed on Amazon,
free downloads of her already published works: for each review, you get a free book.
And
A free copy pre publication copy of all new books…
And
Other neat freebies as they come, from bookmarks to stickers to posters to pens to neat things I find to send out to my betas-
Interested?
Contact Traveler at
travelerpelton@gmail.com for more info…
We would love to add you to the team!

If you enjoy Christian fiction, you might enjoy the series I completed last year called The Oberllyn Family Chronicles. It traces the stories of a single family through three centuries in America, past, preset times and future, with an eye on warning all those of us who love liberty and love the Lord what could happen to our freedoms if we don't guard them and pay attention to what is happening. The first book in the Series, <u>The Oberllyns Overland</u>, deals with the family at the time of the Civil war. *Here's the first couple chapters:*

"Well, mother, it's just about all I can stand," remarked Elijah Oberllyn as he stepped into the kitchen.

"What happened this time?" answered his wife Elizabeth. She was busy rolling out the dough for homemade noodles on the wooden kitchen table. Behind her on the woodstove was bubbling a rich broth to cook them in. From the oven came the wonderful smell of peach pie baking, and warm bread stood on the counter, covered in tea towels. Elizabeth was short woman, with her long black hair, just starting to show grey, done up in a bun at the back of her neck, wearing a solid brown apron over a calico brown dress, and she looked capable of taking on the entire army and feeding it at once. Bustling as she rolled out the dough, she reminded you of a wren on a branch, swaying and hopping from task to task, chirping merrily in between.

"That neighbor Jacks," began her husband. "He's let his cattle get into my wheat again. He says he'll mend the fence but this time he said it was my fault because if I hadn't planted wheat, his cows wouldn't have been tempted, and he is talking about suing me for tempting his cows!"

His wife looked at him and finally said, "You're serious? He is going to try suing you for tempting cows?" She started to laugh out loud but hushed herself when she saw how angry her husband was. "It appears to me the only person to benefit from that would be the lawyers."

"He wants my field to add to his farm. He won't mend the fences on purpose. He's expecting me to do his fence. He's doing the same thing to our son. He offered him a pittance for his orchard, and when Noah wouldn't sell, he started rumors about him being half crazed since the church kicked him out during the great Disappointment and not being right so some of our own neighbors are questioning us for having our own services and I simply am not sure what to do. It's bad enough he picks on us but really, taking off after my son is just about all I can stand." Elizabeth considered for a moment, then said quietly to her husband,

"It's not much of a witness to be fighting with the neighbors. Joe wants to go to California to hunt for gold, but Catherine is not about to drop everything for a wild goose chase. Noah seems content here. I haven't spoken to Mary or Emily about it. I suppose we could consider moving but I hate the idea."

"We've lived here peaceably with our neighbors for years. It's only since those Jacks moved into their uncle's farm we've had trouble. Our land is fertile enough, but when Jacks heard we'd tried to buy his uncle's farm once, he took a dislike to us. And now look." Her husband poured himself a cup of coffee and sat down, blowing on it to cool it, then looking at is wife with a pensive expression on his face.

"California is a right far piece to go," he started.

"Elijah! I was only giving you ideas from different members of the family, not saying I wanted to go." His wife turned with her hands on her hips, a distinctly displeased look on her face.

"It's a good idea and I might have to look into it. I don't want to be run out of town on a rail and that's just what that Jack's fellow is going to try and make happen. Besides, it's getting too crowded around here. It wasn't so bad before that train got put in. Now there are more people coming to buy land and settle in and it's just too crowded."

"Well, you need to pray about anything before you go off half-cocked," she said firmly. "Now go do your chores whilst I finish up supper."

Elijah went back to his barn and finished cleaning out stalls. His wife's jerseys would be up soon for milking. They'd cost him a pretty penny when he'd gotten them, but had proven to be just what Ma's dairy business needed. They gave rich milk, it made wonderful cheese and butter, and their farm was getting known for its good fruit and cheese. Until that neighbor had moved here, everything had been going along fine. Joe had a good thought, though. Out west, there was plenty of land and it wasn't crowded. They could worship as they pleased on Saturday and not be accused of being Judaizers or crazy or anything else. He had two more children at home and there'd be no land to give them as a farm of their own if he couldn't buy up some land. When his son Nathaniel got married, it was a good thing he was a doctor who hadn't time to farm. The farm was just too divided up as it was, what with Emily and her brood, and Catherine and David over by the creek running the small fruits part of the family business. Miriam's man Joe being a lawyer had helped; they'd just needed land for a house and little garden for themselves, no real farming involved. Noah and Mary had taken over the fruit orchard and were making a good go of it, and he and Elizabeth still had enough for him to raise the best horses and oxen in the county and keep mom's dairy running, but they needed more land. It just couldn't be divided anymore and there was Thomas and Johanna yet to be grown and have a part. He supposed Thomas could inherit their home but where would Joanna go? And that Jacks trying to force them to sell land to him they didn't have to spare, he and his dirty tricks. Hard to imagine what he'd try next. Maybe Joe had a good idea. *I believe I'll just visit the land office and find out about land west of here. It surely wouldn't be bad to have a look.*

He came out of the barn and stretched. His son Thomas came dashing up; that child never went anywhere at a walk, always running. "Pa, you got a letter."

"Oh? Thank you, son. Let's have a look." He took the letter from him. It was an official looking document from the US government.

"Haven't seen one of these since well before you were born."

"Was that back when you and mama lived in New York?"

"Yes, pretty much when you were a baby, before grandpa died and we inherited the farm."

"Wonder what they want?"

"Whatever it is, your mom and I will deal with it. You're supposed to have seen to the goats."

"Done. You know the mom angora is going to give birth any day?" he grinned. "Can't wait to see them. I love the way the babies sprong around."

"Well, you keep a good eye on her."

Thomas hesitated. "Pa, I saw Mike Jacks over looking at mom's sheep. He had this funny look on his face?"

"Funny like how?"

"He said his dad doesn't like sheep, they ruin the field. I told him it wasn't his field so not to worry about it. He said something under his breath and walked off. I don't like him much, pa. I was hoping for a friend that would move in that I could do stuff with but I don't think he likes me much."

"Don't worry about him. There are other folks to be with that don't cause such aggravation. Just be civil and leave him be."

"Yes, pa. He made Johanna cry. Oh!" he covered his mouth.

"What?"

"I wasn't supposed to tell you."

"Stop right now. You don't keep secrets from me, ever. When was Johanna crying?"

"She went out to get the cows yesterday and Ellie Jacks was waiting and called her a cowgirl and teased her about her hair."

"What's wrong with her hair?"

"It's sort of red, I guess. And Johanna was crying when she helped with milking."

"I see. And you weren't supposed to tell me?"

"Johanna said we were having enough trouble with this family and God wouldn't want her complaining about it."

"I see. Well, you just let me handle this. Must be about time for supper, yes, there's mom ringing the dinner bell. Let's go wash up."

Dad and Thomas washed up at the pump and went inside, hanging their hats by the door.

"That smell sure chirks a fellow up, ma. Can't wait to have some of your chicken and noodles." Elizabeth smiled.

"Johanna, would you mind getting the field tea I made? I put it in the springhouse to get cold." Johanna nodded and went out the door, coming back with a pitcher covered in a towel.

" Mom," she frowned. "I don't think we ought to use the tea."

"What's the matter?"

"Somebody's been in the spring house."

"Really? How do you know?"

"The cheese's are all on the floor and the milk's spilt." Ma and Pa rushed outside to the spring house where they found rounds of cheese scattered all over, the five gallon milk cans flipped, polluting the spring run over. They looked around at the damage. Ma shook her head.

"I hate to think we'd have to put guards on our home, but this is outrageous."

"If we tell the sheriff," began Thomas.

"He'll say it could've been done by animals, that someone left the door open. There's no proof."

"Why don't we make a list of what's going on at least and ask him to watch out with us?" asked Ma.

"We can do that. Are the cheeses ruined?"

"The shelves are broken down, but the cheese ought to be fine. I may have to rewrap some.."

"Let's see what we can do. Thomas - call Mick and Mike." Mike and Mick were the family mastiffs who spent most the time in the back field with the cattle. The dogs came to Thomas's call. "We'd best keep the dogs close to the yard or at least one of them here."

"Then who's going to protect the cattle from coyotes?" asked Thomas.

"It's not the four legged ones I am worried about just now."

Thomas and dad reset the shelves, and they helped mom wipe off the wax coated cheeses and set them back. While they did that, mom set the milk cans up and opened the overflow wide so the water could drain out and run clear. Finally they stood up and went out. Dad shut the door to the spring house and set Mike by the door, telling him to stay. He took Mick to the barn and set him there and they went inside to eat.

The meal was a quiet one. Ma and Pa were tight-lipped and Thomas and Johanna were quiet as they passed food around.

"I don't care what they say. Johanna, you have got the prettiest hair in the world. It shines in the sun like gold and when you wear your green Sabbath dress I have the prettiest sister in the county."

Johanna looked surprised and her eyes welled up. "Thank you," she whispered.

"I agree with your brother. I am not quite sure why he said it but thank you for noticing," said Pa. Mom and Johanna just looked confused. Suddenly, there was a loud meow from out back.

"What on earth!" said Ma, getting up. She went out back where a strange collie dog had her pet cat up a tree. She took a switch and chased it off. The dog ran to the end of the driveway where Mike Jacks was watching.

"Lady, you'd better not hurt my dog," he yelled at her.

"Then keep him on your own land," she replied.

"Well, this is going to be our land when my dad gets done with you," he yelled back. "You'd better not let those sheep overgraze it." Mom picked up a bigger switch and headed down the drive purposefully in his direction and he ran off. A passing wagon stopped.

"You all right, Mrs. Oberllyn?" said the farmer driving.

"I don't know, Zeb. We got neighbor problems. My spring house was attacked, they insult us and we just never did them any harm."

"I heard about some of that. Mr. Jacks was in the general store last week boasting he'd have your land soon. I don't know what he was talking about but I was coming to tell your husband if he was going to sell out, to call on me. I could use good fields like yours."

"I thank you, and I'll tell Elijah, but we have no interest in leaving our farm. It's been in the family for over a hundred years."

"Thought he might be blowing smoke. But still, keep me and my sons in mind. I'd rather buy from you than Jacks. Oh, and best be careful. There's some weird rumors going around." Elijah was on the porch and waved to his neighbor.

"Rumors?"

"I'm sure they ain't true. You say howdy to Elijah for me."

"Thank you, Zeb. By the way, did he happen to say why he wanted my land?"

"He said it was the best land in the district and I have to agree with him. Your orchards make the best fruit, your cheese is wonderful and you've always been real supportive of our community. Shame to have you leave."

"Aren't planning on leaving.."

"I hope not. Well, I best be getting home. You remember my offer."

Mom went to the back where Thomas had climbed the tree and gotten her Maine coon cat down. He jumped into her arms. "There, there, dear. I'm sorry he flustered you so. Shh, now. Shhh."

"Mom, why do they hate us?"

"I have no idea." They went inside. "We've never had this much trouble."

"Mom, did you know Jacks have got slaves?"

"What?"

"They have three of them. I saw them out working his field. And Mr. Jacks carries a whip."

"I see. Well, the good Lord never wanted slavery. We earn our needs by the works of our hands, not the sweat of others. Let's try to finish supper. It's most likely all cold by now."

Bibliography if you want to go research habits....

Bayley PJ, Frascino JC, Squire LR. Robust habit learning in the absence of awareness and independent of the medial temporal lobe. Nature. 2005;436(7050):550–555

Gardner B, de Bruijn GJ, Lally P. A systematic review and meta-analysis of applications of the Self-Report Habit Index to nutrition and physical activity behaviours. Ann Behav Med. 2011;42(2):174–187

Hull CL. Principles of behavior: an introduction to behavior theory. New York, NY: Appleton-Century-Crofts; 1943.

Inzlicht, M., Bartholow, B., & Hirsh, J. (2015). Emotional foundations of cognitive control. *Trends in Cognitive Sciences, 19*, 126–132.

Kahneman D. A perspective on judgment and choice. Am Psychol. 2003;58(9):697–720.

Lally P, Gardner B. Promoting habit formation. Health Psychol Rev. In press: DOI: 10.1080/17437199.2011.603604

Lally P, van Jaarsveld CHM, Potts HWW, Wardle J. How are habits formed: modelling habit formation in the real world. Euro J Soc Psychol. 2010;40:998–1009.

Lally P, Wardle J, Gardner B. Experiences of habit formation: a qualitative study. Psychol Health Med. 2011;16(4):484–489.

Neal DT, Wood W, Labrecque JS, Lally P. How do habits guide behavior? Perceived and actual triggers of habits in daily life. J Exp Soc Psychol. 2012;48:492–498.

Schonberg, T., Bakkour, A., Hover, A. M., Mumford, J. A., Nagar, L., Perez, J., & Poldrack, R. A. (2014). Changing value through cued approach: An automatic mechanism of behavior change. *Nature Neuroscience, 17*, 625–630.

Wood W, Neal DT. A new look at habits and the habit-goal interface. Psychol Rev. 2007;114(4):843–863.
12.

A smile costs nothing, but gives much-
It takes but a moment, but the memory of it usually lasts forever.
 None are so rich that can get along without it-
And none are so poor but that can be made rich by it.

 It enriches those who receive,
without making poor those who give-
It creates sunshine in the home,
Fosters good will in business,
And is the best antidote for trouble-
And yet it cannot be begged, borrowed, or stolen,
for it is of no value
Unless it is given away.

 Some people are too busy to give you a smile-
Give them one of yours-
For the good Lord knows that no one needs a smile so badly
As he or she who has no more smiles left to give.
 ~ Author Unknown

Lightning Source UK Ltd.
Milton Keynes UK
UKHW040820240819
348427UK00029B/121/P